MAKING BETTER BUSINESS DECISIONS

MAKING BETTER BUSINESS DECISIONS

Understanding and Improving Critical Thinking and Problem-Solving Skills

Steve W. Williams
Texas Southern University

 Sage Publications
International Educational and Professional Publisher
Thousand Oaks ▪ London ▪ New Delhi

For information:

Sage Publications, Inc.
2455 Teller Road
Thousand Oaks, California 91320
E-mail: order@sagepub.com

Sage Publications Ltd.
6 Bonhill Street
London EC2A 4PU
United Kingdom

Sage Publications India Pvt. Ltd.
M-32 Market
Greater Kailash I
New Delhi 110 048 India

Printed in the United States of America

Library of Congress Cataloging-in-Publication Data

Williams, Steve W.
  Making better business decisions: Understanding and improving
critical thinking and problem-solving skills / By Steve W. Williams.
      p. cm.
Includes bibliographical references and index.
  ISBN 0-7619-2421-3 (cloth) — ISBN 0-7619-2422-1 (pbk.)
  1. Decision making. 2. Problem solving. I. Title.
  HD30.23 .W538 2002
  658.4'03—dc21   2001006047

01   02   03   04   05   10   9   8   7   6   5   4   3   2   1

Acquiring Editor: Marquita Flemming
Editorial Assistant: MaryAnn Vail
Production Editor: Diane S. Foster
Editorial Assistant: Candice Crosetti
Copy Editor: Jackie Tasch
Typesetter/Designer: Denyse Dunn
Proofer: Scott Oney
Indexer: Molly Hall
Cover Designer: Jane Quaney

Contents

List of Tables

List of Figures

1 | Introduction

We are faced with hundreds of decisions every day. We chose when to get up this morning, what clothing we would wear, and even whether to read this book. Most of the consequences of the decisions we make throughout our day are relatively trivial or inconsequential. It probably didn't matter too much if we decided to sleep an extra 15 minutes this morning or if we selected the blue shirt rather than the green one. However, some of the decisions we make can carry substantial consequences. Choosing to get an undergraduate or graduate degree, deciding on a new job or career, or selecting one vendor out of many candidates to be our company's long-term supplier of a necessary resource are important decisions that are likely to have a significant and meaningful impact on our lives. Learning, understanding, and applying critical thinking and creative problem-solving skills can improve the quality of the decisions that mean the most to us.

Many of our decisions don't need much thought. Relatively small, routine, or mundane choices generally don't require us to spend a lot of time or energy because the outcomes associated with these types of decisions probably don't affect us very much. In other cases, however, we need to spend time to *think* about our decisions, especially those related to solving problems.

Important decisions can shape our lives, and our decision quality is improved if we critically and creatively analyze the problems facing us by considering new and different options, weighing the evidence objectively, looking at a problem from a different angle that gives us different insights, developing novel solutions that effectively solve our dilemmas, and accurately forecasting the probable impact of our decisions.

To think critically and solve problems creatively, we must first understand how decisions are made and the factors influencing our decision-making processes. Much of what is taught through formal education concerns how decisions *should* be made. Although an understanding of rational decision making helps to explain decisional processes, behavioral decision theory is concerned with how people actually *do* make decisions. If we as decision makers are aware of the factors influencing both our interpretation of problems and the methods we use to solve them, then we are better able to see subjective patterns of behavior in our own decision actions and take steps to minimize and avoid their possible negative impact on what we decide. If we are aware of how the mind processes information and how biological, physiological, and psychological factors influence thinking, we are better prepared to address their probable influence on our decisions. And if we are aware of conceptual blocks that hinder our creativity and innovation, then we are better able to overcome their constraining effects and unleash the creative potential in our minds.

Do you have trouble making decisions? If so, you're not alone. Most of us find decision making difficult, as the list in Table 1.1 demonstrates. This book distills what behavioral science has discovered related to how people, especially those in business, make decisions. Findings presented here are derived from supportive research representing what we currently know about decision making and problem solving. The information presented in the following chapters should enable decision makers to recognize and focus on the truly important decisions that require critical thinking, to analyze options more clearly and creatively, to reduce decisional time and effort, and to improve judgment quality. Awareness and application of the material contained here not only will enable us to improve our own decisions, but also will provide the means for us to understand how and why others decide as they do.

Critical thinking is a process that emphasizes a rational basis for what we believe and provides standards and procedures for analyzing, testing, and evaluating our beliefs (Rudinow & Barry, 1994). Critical thinking skills enable decision makers to define problems within the proper context, to examine evidence objectively, and to analyze the assumptions underlying the evidence and our own beliefs. Critical thinking enables us to

TABLE 1.1 Decision-Making Difficulty

Type of Decision	Percentage of People Who Have Trouble Making This Type of Decision
Making political choices	76
Buying life insurance	73
Choosing the best school for their children	72
Buying a new car	71
Selecting clothing to wear	63
Planning how to lose weight	61
Choosing a doctor	55
Deciding where to vacation	52

SOURCE: Data are drawn from *U.S. News and World Report*, February 5, 1990, p. 74.

understand and deal with the positions of others and to clarify and comprehend our own thoughts as well. When critical thinking is applied, all aspects of the decision process are involved, from defining the problem, identifying and weighing decision criteria, and generating and evaluating alternatives to estimating the consequences that will result from our decisions. However, critical thinking does *not* mean that we always make the best possible decision, never reach the wrong conclusion, and never make mistakes; it is simply a process we apply that enables us to arrive at superior decisions consistently.

Creativity results in the production of novel or new ideas (Amabile, 1988). *Creativity* means doing things differently: being unique, clever, innovative, or original. Creative solutions are those that aren't limited by self-imposed boundaries, those that consider the full spectrum of options from logical to seemingly illogical, and those that result in the creation of new and improved ways of doing things.

Critical thinking involves determining what we know and why we know it; *creativity* involves generating, considering, and using new ideas, concepts, and solutions. Applied together, the two strategies enable decision makers to analyze objectively and reason out the situation facing them and to come up with different and potentially unexpected ways of addressing and correcting problems.

This introduction provides some background information and offers an example of the *rational decision process:* the method generally believed to be used by decision makers and the method our education system teaches us to apply. However, rational decision making rarely occurs in the real world, at least for most of the complex, complicated, and unique problems facing business decision makers. To the extent we are able to meet the assumptions underlying the application of the rational process, our decisions approach optimality, but these ideal circumstances rarely (if ever) occur. Instead, we tend to shortcut the process and latch onto the first potential solution that meets our minimum expectations so we can move on to the next problem facing us in our busy lives.

Part I of this text lays the foundation for understanding the many internal factors that influence our decisions. As living beings, we have a host of biological, emotional, and psychological processes that (often without our knowledge) affect how we make decisions, and the chapters in this section analyze how these elements alter and distort our thinking ability. Part II focuses on understanding how we know what we know. The chapters in this section explore the elements of critical thinking: our attitude and belief infrastructure, which sets in motion our interpretation of what we hear, considering the source of information presented to us, weighing alternative explanations for what we are told, and testing the facts as we understand them. Part III deals with thinking creatively. In these chapters, a framework for creativity is offered, the stages of creativity are presented, and creativity-enhancing techniques are discussed.

Many of the decisions we make and the problems we face don't require much in the way of critical thinking or creativity. Applying rational decision techniques or intuition can most likely solve our everyday routine, repetitive, and minor problems. Using rules of thumb or general guidelines can speed up the decision process, and the results are generally "good enough" for the current situation—thinking critically and solving problems creatively take time and effort, and we should apply these scarce resources where they are most needed. As decisions become more important and problems become more difficult, the energy required by critical thinking skills and creative problem solving can improve the quality of our thought processes and increase the likelihood of uncovering optimal solutions.

If not all decisions require us to be critical in our thinking and creative in our problem solving, how are we to know when to apply these skills? To understand when the use of critical thinking skills and creative problem-solving techniques will be most beneficial, we need to know something about the type of decision to be made, and we need to understand how decisions *should* be made under perfect conditions. If we subjected every decision we made to what is known as the rational decision process, we would end up with the best, most optimal solution all the time. Of course, this would also mean that we would make very few decisions and that we would spend most of our time attempting to solve problems and very little time actually implementing solutions. Under ideal conditions (in other words, not in the real world), problem solving should model the following steps.

THE RATIONAL DECISION PROCESS

If decision makers had access to all the relevant information they needed, had enough time and energy to reach the best possible solution, and were unimpeded by "being human," they would always use the rational decision process. All of us strive to make the best decisions we can, but we are usually limited by certain constraints. Sometimes, we don't have enough information or enough time, or we just aren't sure what we need to do to develop an optimal answer. We would like to make the most reasonable, logical, and objective decision possible, but we are seldom able to arrive at an optimal solution. Most of the time, to the extent possible, we try to be as rational as we can by using what economists term the rational decision-making process, a problem-solving approach that involves the following sequence of events: problem identification, criteria definition, alternative generation and evaluation, and implementation (see Figure 1.1).

Problem identification. To come up with a rational solution, decision makers must first recognize that a problem exists. This sounds obvious, but research has demonstrated that problem definition is not as straightforward as it would seem. Is a 5% sales decrease a problem? What about a 2% decline? Is a 20% increase a problem if our company has limited production capacity? Rarely are the situations we confront clearly labeled as *problem* or *nonproblem.* In addition, people can distort, ignore, omit, and discount information to such an extent that they often deny they are

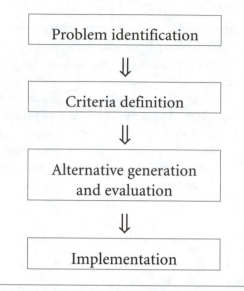

Figure 1.1. The Rational Decision Process

faced with a problem (Cowan, 1986). Managers with a morale problem in their department may convince themselves that the situation isn't quite as bad as some believe, or even that the symptoms they witness are related to something else entirely and no problem exists. Cultural factors have also been found to influence the extent to which individuals perceive a situation as a problem. For example, an American manager might define a notice from a prime supplier that necessary construction materials will be 3 months late as a problem, whereas a more situation-accepting Asian manager might not call the identical situation a problem because Asian cultures are more likely to believe that the outcome is simply fate or God's will (Adler, 1997).

Criteria definition. Most problems are multidimensional, and decision makers must determine what factors should be considered to resolve the problem they are facing. Perfectly rational decision makers would identify all the relevant criteria that might influence the decision process. The range of possible objectives for a specific problem might include price, quality, features, dependability, reputation, and so on. If certain criteria are not identified as relevant, then they have no impact on the subsequent decision process. Once the important criteria are found, the decision maker needs to recognize that not all of the factors are equally important to problem resolution. For example, people are often willing to sacrifice higher quality to gain a lower price. A difficulty many problem solvers face is that they fail to take into account an important criterion when considering their options, or they allow irrelevant criteria to influence their judgment. Although we might initially think service availability is unimportant when we make our decision to purchase office computers, we may later discover that on-site maintenance is critical after an employee experiences a computer breakdown. Or we may have identified all the important decision criteria correctly, but then we allow irrelevant factors such as persuasive sales pressure or emotional appeal to sway our judgment unduly.

Alternative generation and evaluation. At this stage, the decision maker identifies all the possible courses of action and evaluates each alternative against the established criteria. A rational decision maker would generate a list of all possible alternatives that are likely to resolve the problem and proceed to weigh the advantages and disadvantages of each. Fully rational decision makers assess the possible consequences of selecting a given alternative for each of the identified criteria, resulting in a ranking of possible solutions from most likely to resolve the problem (or the best possible solution) down to the least likely. Generating a full range of possibilities is extremely important because research has demonstrated that the quality of the final solution can be significantly improved by considering as many alternatives as possible (Maier, 1970). Rational evaluation involves considering the extent to which applying a particular solution will create additional difficulties, the extent to which those involved in the outcome will accept and be able to implement the alternative, and the extent to which the alternative considers organizational constraints and additional external factors.

Implementation. Once the optimal option has been discovered, the final step involves implementing and following up on the solution. Many decisions, especially those in organizations, require the assistance of others (those who didn't make the decision) to carry them out. Implementation concerns getting the commitment of those needed to achieve the objective and monitoring to be sure that correct implementation occurs.

Expecting a solution to be successfully implemented by participants who fail to support or even disagree with the objective is likely to be unrealistic. Again, studies demonstrate that commitment to and implementation of the solution are enhanced to the extent those responsible for implementation participate in the decision process and accept the given solution (Locke & Latham, 1988). Implementation also involves acquiring feedback to determine whether the solution adequately resolved the problem and the overall effectiveness of the solution.

AN EXAMPLE OF THE
RATIONAL DECISION PROCESS

Problem identification. To demonstrate how the rational decision process should work, consider how a manager would decide which brand of vehicles would best meet the needs of the company. The first step is to recognize that a problem exists: how to deliver our product to our customers. Notice that the problem statement dictates to a large degree what criteria and alternatives will be considered in the following phases. Asking how we can best deliver our products is a different question from asking what type of vehicle we should purchase. The range of options a manager might consider related to delivering products is much broader than those the manager would deem necessary for selecting an appropriate vehicle. For example, alternatives for delivering products might include leasing transportation, subcontracting delivery to a carrier service, and using public transportation, as well as the possibility of buying a fleet of delivery vans. Let's assume that the manager has considered all viable ways to identify the given situation and has correctly analyzed the problem as the need to purchase a number of delivery vehicles.

Criteria definition. Now, the manager needs to come up with the objectives that are important when considering the type and quantity of vehicles to buy. A thoroughly rational decision maker would develop an exhaustive list of all possible criteria and rank each factor as to its degree of importance. Table 1.2 shows how a scale of 1 to 10 might be used to weight criteria importance for this example. When considering how many and what kind of transportation vehicles the company requires, the manager might think that size, fuel economy, comfort, safety, cost,

TABLE 1.2 Possible Criteria Weighting

Criterion	Weight (from 10 to 1)
Initial price	10
Fuel economy	8
Durability	8
Performance	7
Interior comfort	4

reliability, and a host of other considerations are important. Once the criteria have been developed, the relative value of each will have to be determined. Is price more important than size? Is fuel economy more critical than comfort? How much will each vehicle carry, and how many will be required? Does reliability carry more weight than safety, and so forth.

Alternative generation and evaluation. With the relative importance of all criteria in mind, the manager will then come up with a list of possible manufacturers and the extent to which the products they offer satisfy the relevant criteria. The offerings of automobile makers such as Ford, Chevrolet, Toyota, Honda, and so on will need to be learned, and each possibility will have to be carefully assessed against the established standards. If price, availability, and fuel economy are the most important factors, how do the different styles rank? If the manager discovers all possible vehicles, weighs the possibilities against all possible criteria, and ranks the results, the optimal choice should be obvious. An example of the weighting for four possible vehicles is shown in Table 1.3, and Table 1.4 presents the final ranking of the four choices.

Implementation. Now that the manager knows which van will meet the company's needs and how many are required, the actual purchase needs to occur. The extent to which this solution resolves the identified problem needs to be determined. Does the purchase of this line of vehicles adequately solve the problem of delivering our products to our customers? Has the resolution been implemented correctly, and do any modifications or corrections need to be made?

TABLE 1.3 Examples of Decision Criteria Weighting

Alternative	Initial Price	Fuel Economy	Durability	Performance	Interior Comfort
Vehicle 1	5	6	10	7	10
Vehicle 2	7	8	5	7	6
Vehicle 3	2	7	10	4	9
Vehicle 4	10	7	3	5	3

To the extent that the manager exhaustively followed the procedures outlined above, the quality of the decision solution approaches the optimal. Unfortunately, decision makers rarely have the time, means, and cognitive abilities to apply the rational decision process. For example, problems are often identified in terms of the solution. In fact, we often bias our judgments of the strengths and weaknesses of the alternatives we consider to make them fit with the way we've identified the problem (Langer & Schank, 1994). If the company is experiencing a decrease in productivity, a manager might identify the problem as "We have to get rid of Joe because he's lazy and incompetent." Joe may indeed be the cause of a lack of performance, but the rational decision process will only derive an optimal solution to the extent that the "real" problem is identified. "How can we replace Joe?" is a fundamentally different problem than "How can we improve productivity?" As the purchasing example above demonstrated, identifying a delivery problem in terms of the need to buy trucks frames the problem in terms of the solution, which narrows the range of alternatives the decision maker will generate and consider in an attempt to resolve the identified problem. Defining the problem too narrowly or, worse yet, defining the wrong problem will result in a poorer outcome. As folk wisdom indicates, "It isn't the things you don't know that get you into trouble, but the things you know for sure that aren't so." Problems that are stated clearly and do not contain unwarranted assumptions or preconceived biases greatly influence our ability to optimize solutions. To the extent decision makers identify and frame problems correctly, the rational decision process works very well in leading to the best possible result.

TABLE 1.4 Assessment of Alternatives

Alternative	Initial Price	Fuel Economy	Durability	Performance	Interior Comfort	Totals
Vehicle 1	50	48	80	49	40	267
Vehicle 2	70	64	40	49	24	247
Vehicle 3	20	56	80	28	36	220
Vehicle 4	100	56	24	35	12	227

NOTE: In this table, the weighting values from Table 1.2 are multiplied by the data in Table 1.3 to provide final values.

If the real problem has been correctly and accurately identified, the best solution still may not be selected if the right criteria are not considered. If we have identified the problem as the need to purchase delivery vehicles, we will not be able to determine which of the many possible brands will best meet our needs if we fail to include all the criteria that could influence our judgment. We might evaluate the complete range of delivery vehicle brands available based on price, quality, fuel economy, and dependability but fail to consider the accessibility of parts for repair as an important factor. Only after we've bought our fleet of vans do we discover that repairs are difficult because replacement parts have to be shipped from the other side of the globe; if we had included the service criterion in our original list (or at least considered it more thoroughly), we would likely have made a different (and one can hope a more optimal) decision. On a more personal level, anyone who has gone through the car-buying process knows how automobile salespeople target transient or rationally irrelevant criteria in an attempt to get you to purchase the vehicle of their choice, not yours. You may have gone to the car dealer completely prepared with your list of relevant criteria indicating what was important to you in a family car: price, comfort, affordability, economy, and so forth. However, the salesperson is able to target your impulsive side by having you take the two-door speedster for a test drive, and you end up with a red convertible instead of the station wagon you meant to buy. Critical thinking skills greatly increase our ability to identify problems and develop relevant criteria.

Even if the decision maker does an excellent job of properly identifying the problem and developing and ranking all the relevant judgmental criteria, the best solution may not be achieved if the optimal possibility is not included as one of the possible solutions. In fact, many times we even fail to consider all of the alternatives we have generated because we make up our minds about the "right" decision quite early and then massage information to support our implicit favorite and convince ourselves that further consideration is unnecessary because the already-made decision was the correct one (Langer & Schank, 1994). If we have correctly identified the problem as the need to purchase delivery vehicles and accurately listed our weighted criteria, we will not be able to determine the best possible brand if we are unaware that it is a viable option or if we distort our beliefs about other candidates to justify our preferred choice. To solve our delivery vehicle problem, we generate a list of all vehicles manufactured by Ford, General Motors, and Chrysler but are unaware that Hyundai makes a commercial delivery van that suits our needs admirably. Or we consider all cargo vans but fail to include the full range of possibilities, such as other types of transportation: semitrailers and covered trucks. Or we have a preferred alternative because we prefer Ford products and fail to give subsequent options serious consideration because this predecision deemphasizes the other options (Power & Aldag, 1985).

An even more disastrous outcome would be if we selected the best delivery van, but the solution created greater problems due to unforeseen consequences, such as a lack of enough parking space to house the fleet on arrival or an inability to find enough qualified drivers to operate the vans due to a need for specialized expertise. All possible alternatives must take into account both short- and long-term consequences; it does little good to solve the immediate problem but create a more difficult situation later on. It is primarily in the area of alternative generation that creativity can have the greatest impact on decision making.

The rational decision process has been successfully followed and the optimal solution has been found, but even the best answer may not resolve the problem if it is implemented incorrectly. After careful and thorough consideration, the optimal resolution of our delivery vehicle problem is discovered to be a fleet of Korean cargo vans. Rationally, the vehicles appear to be the "best" choice. However, certain factions within the vehicle maintenance department hold strong pro-American views and believe the company's decision to purchase foreign vehicles is "unpatriotic," and they are less than enthusiastic about seeing the new line achieve success. This lack of support manifests itself in decreased efficiency and even episodes of sabotage. To determine whether the solution has actually solved the identified problem, feedback needs to be gathered and assessed. Do the new cargo vans resolve our dilemma of how to ship our product to the customer? Does the solution generate any unforeseen complications? Has the situation been altered in some way that results in a different problem or in a less effective solution? Often, the "best" solution in the business world may be not the one that generates the most profit but instead the choice that maximizes the chances that the strategy will be accepted and completely implemented.

THE RATIONAL DECISION PROCESS

In December of 2000, Motor Trend magazine announced that it would select a winner of the Motor Trend 2001 Sport Utility Vehicle Award, a prestigious and highly sought after honor. Of the dozens of sport utility vehicles manufactured, only all-new or substantially revised SUVs available in North America by January 1, 2001, were eligible for consideration, and 12 candidates were selected for testing. The 12 vehicles were compared according to their design, engineering, performance, interior, special features, safety, off-road capability, and value.

Motor Trend's comments about the rational decision process? "Twelve vehicles. 10 editors (not to mention two photographers, plus our own road test and TV crews). Weeks of testing. Hundreds of gallons of gas. At least a gross of fast-food burgers, plus enough road snacks to feed an army. Long days and late nights." The winner? Acura's MDX at almost $40,000.

—Motor Trend (December 2000, pp. 35-57)

Here's a story about an employee who was faced with a tough choice. Although objective criteria favored one option, his intuition prompted him in another direction, and he couldn't make up his mind. After agonizing about the proper course of action, he finally took the problem to his boss. She listened attentively to his description of the situation and said,

Well, first of all, make sure you've identified the problem correctly. Once you've done that, develop a list of all pertinent criteria and weight them according to importance. Then generate as many alternative solutions as you can and compare each to your standards, keeping in mind that the rest of us will have to implement whatever you decide. After you've finished the process, you should have the best solution.

The employee chuckled at the manager's suggestion and replied, "No, really, this is a *serious* problem." Although the rational decision process may sound appealing, many of us feel that "serious" problem solving should somehow involve more: perhaps instinct, intuition, and gut reaction.

The rational decision process makes some fundamental assumptions about how decision makers gather and look at problem-solving information (see Figure 1.2). Under complete rationality, decision makers see problems clearly and unambiguously, and they have complete information regarding the decision situation. Possible solutions will lead to a single, well-defined goal, presenting no conflicts with other goals while allowing a maximal payoff. All criteria and alternatives can be identified, ranking preferences are clear and unchanging, and the decision maker is aware of all possible consequences associated with each. Time and resources are abundantly available to pursue various possibilities and to contemplate probable outcomes. However, most of the problems we face in the real world don't meet the required conditions to allow complete rationality (March, 1994).

Complete application of the sequence of problem identification, criteria definition, alternative generation and evaluation, and implementation as outlined above will invariably result in an optimal solution. Why don't we use the rational decision process all the time if it will lead to the best result? Decision makers, especially business people who rarely have enough time or resources to accomplish all they desire to do, don't particularly like problems. Problems amount to frustration: Things aren't going the way we would like for them to go—something is interfering with our goal attainment. Our natural tendency is to select the first reasonable solution that seems to resolve the current situation (March & Simon, 1958). Unfortunately, the first solution that meets our needs often isn't the optimal solution or even one of the better alternatives.

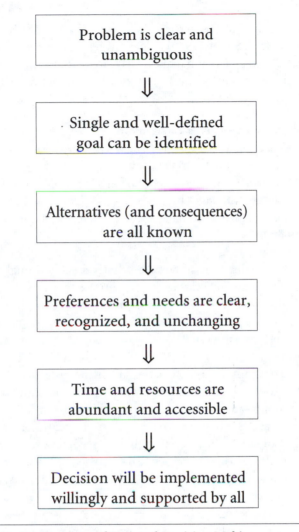

Figure 1.2. Assumptions of Rational Decision Making

BOUNDED RATIONALITY

Nobel prize-winning author Herbert Simon has suggested that business decision makers are constrained from making the best possible decisions due to very real limitations in their thinking abilities (March & Simon, 1958; Simon, 1957). Simon (1990) coined the term *bounded rationality* to explain that although decision makers strive to be fully rational (to make the best or most optimal decision), they are limited or bounded by a number of factors:

1. A lack of complete or fully accurate information
2. A scarcity of the time and resources required to search for more information and to formulate a full spectrum of options
3. An inability to retain more than a small amount of relevant information in the memory to attack the problem
4. Intelligence and perceptual limitations that inhibit the ability to calculate optimal outcomes

Given these constraints, decision makers "satisfice" or willingly accept a decision that is reasonable rather than continue to search for the best possible solution (March & Simon, 1958). We tend to implement solutions that are satisfactory or marginally acceptable instead of looking for the ideal or perfect response.

Even though boundedly rational problem solving leads to systematic errors in our decisions, we usually prefer satisficing instead of continuing to seek out the optimal solution. Why? Many if not most times, a solution that is good enough adequately and cheaply addresses our needs, whereas more elaborate and thorough approaches are unduly expensive and time-consuming (Conlisk, 1996). Decision makers recognize that a trade-off exists between thinking and accuracy (Pitz & Sachs, 1984). Consequently, we identify problems by lumping them with previous problems that seem similar, we limit our criteria to those we believe are most important, we rank the criteria based on our own preferences and self-interests, we come up with very few alternatives, we start with our preferred option and assess our alternatives one at a time against the criteria, we evaluate possibilities until we find one that is sufficient and satisfactory, and we allow corporate politics and power related to implementation to sway our judgments while failing to measure all the decision's possible results (see Table 1.5).

Rational decision making is a time-consuming, systematic process. The reality of business life is that we don't have the time, energy, or resources to use the rational process for most of the hundreds of decisions

TABLE 1.5 Comparing Rational Decision Making and Bounded Rationality

Decision-Making Step	Rational Decision Making	Bounded Rationality
Problem definition	Real problem is identified	Problem primarily reflects the decision maker's interests, understanding, and needs
Criteria definition	All relevant criteria are identified and weighted appropriately	Limited criteria are identified, and evaluation is influenced by self-interest
Alternative generation and evaluation	All options are considered, and all consequences are understood and taken into consideration	Limited options are identified, favored option is given priority, and consideration halts when a "good enough" solution is found
Implementation	All participants understand and support the solution	Politics, power, and self-interest influence the amount of acceptance and commitment to the solution

we face every day. For example, managers perform a different activity about every 9 minutes while at work (Mintzberg, 1975). We are simply unable to do our jobs if we attempt to be too analytical and too thorough, so we prefer to use intuitive judgment whenever possible. Businesspeople reach a speedy outcome by using simplifying strategies or rules of thumb to assist them in their decisional endeavors, and these standards work well most of the time. Painstaking application of the rational thinking process should be reserved for when decisional outcomes are of increasing importance. Even though we are constrained by many of the limitations discussed above, the closer we approximate the rational model, the more likely our decisions will approach the optimal. However, several factors affect not only our ability to make rational decisions but the intuitive rules of thumb we use as well. These internal influences on decision making will be the focus of Part I.

The rational decision process involves defining the problem, developing criteria, generating and evaluating alternatives, and implementing our decisions. It works very well under those conditions in which we have the time, resources, and willingness to practice it properly. Although it is unlikely we can ever apply the rational process completely, we can improve the effectiveness of our use of this approach if we consider the possibilities suggested in Table 1.6 (Whetton & Cameron, 1991).

SUMMARY AND REVIEW

This section introduced us to the *rational decision process,* which is a decision-making model stressing the thorough evaluation of all components of a decision. When using rational decision making, we would define the problem, identify and weight criteria that are important to the problem, generate and evaluate a comprehensive list of alternative solutions to the problem, and finally, implement our solution and follow up on it to assure that the problem has been resolved. Unfortunately, although decision makers strive to reach optimal solutions, we are generally unable to execute the rational process to its fullest extent. Decision makers are constrained by bounded rationality, a host of human limitations that lead us to satisfice or willingly settle on a solution that is good enough rather than seeking the best outcome possible.

TABLE 1.6 Effective Use of Rational Problem Solving

When Defining the Problem

- Differentiate facts from opinions
- Specify underlying causes and symptoms
- Be as explicit as possible in stating the problem
- Identify any violated standards or expectations
- Determine who actually owns the problem
- Avoid stating the problem in terms of a solution
- Encourage participation of those involved

When Identifying and Weighting Criteria

- Be as complete as possible in recognizing relevant criteria
- Maintain objectivity when weighting criteria
- Recognize that criteria that are not explicitly stated become irrelevant to the subsequent decision
- Be aware of how personal preferences influence criteria

When Generating and Evaluating Alternatives

- Postpone evaluating alternatives until completing the generation process
- Allow those who will be influenced by the decision to be involved
- Bear in mind the results desired and specify alternatives that are consistent with desired results
- Build on the ideas of others
- Be systematic and evaluate all options
- Compare to both desired results and an optimal standard
- Keep in mind potential side effects and weaknesses
- Be explicit in stating selected alternative

When Implementing and Following Up

- Be aware of implementation timing
- Provide opportunities for feedback from those involved
- Gain the acceptance of those affected by the decision as much as possible
- Establish a monitoring system to provide feedback
- Evaluate based on problem solution rather than side benefits

Part I

Internal Influences on Decision Making

2 | Biological Factors Influencing Decisions

Better decisions come from understanding how emotional and physiological responses brought about by the environmental conditions we are experiencing govern our thought processes. Emotions and reactions can override our attempts to be rational. On the other hand, people have the amazing capacity of directing their attention and taking control of their impulsive nature when they realize that the expenditure is worth the effort. Part of being a human decision maker is realizing that biological factors have a continual and often unnoticed influence on how we solve problems.

Our unbelievably complex yet elegantly simple human brain is the best organized, most functional three pounds of matter in the known universe (Sylwester, 1995). Recent research aided by technological advancements such as brain imaging has improved our understanding of how biochemical processes influence the brain's ability to make decisions. Even though our rational cortical forebrain stands alone when compared to other brains within the animal kingdom in terms of size and capabilities, findings indicate that the primitive subcortical emotional and survival elements have powerful influences on what we think and how we act. The biochemical processes of our bodies can influence our decisions.

The brain is made up of tens of billions of nerve cells, called neurons, which are highly interconnected (Sylwester, 1995). These neurons are so tiny that 30,000 of them would barely fill a pinhead. The neurons of the brain interact electrochemically with each other and with distant body cells through an extremely complex system of tubular extensions that send and receive messages. Through this chemical connection, any given neuron is only a few neurons away from all the cells in the body, and this highly interconnected system of neurons is recognized as the principal agent of what we call cognition or thinking (Kimmelberg & Norenberg, 1989). Information is passed along this intricate highway by more than 50 chemical molecules (for example, amino acids, monoamines, and peptides), which are called *neurotransmitters* (Novitt-Moreno, 1995). Many of these neurotransmitters play a very important role in moderating our emotional states and our problem-solving ability.

One example of how neurotransmitters affect our behavior is how cortisol (a peptide) activates physiological reactions to perceived stress. Humans are wired with what is commonly called the "fight or flight" response. When we perceive stress, our bodies gear up to provide us with either the capability to fight the source of the stress or, more commonly, the additional resources required to run away and fight another day. However, this stress response, which helps protect our bodies from danger, fails to differentiate between physical and emotional problems. Rarely do we encounter an event at the workplace that is physically dangerous or life threatening. Most situations that cause us stress are psychological and ongoing rather than physical and immediate.

When we experience a stressor, whether the source of that stress is a cut, a virus, an unexpected loud noise, or an overload at work, the body reacts by signaling the pituitary gland (about the size of a cherry at the base of the brain) to send a hormonal message to the adrenals to release cortisol (and other hormones) into our system (Selye, 1956). Once cortisol enters the bloodstream, it triggers a succession of chemical changes in the body: Stored sugar is released into the system (as a source of energy), blood coagulants are activated (in case the stressor can physically damage us), and digestive processes are halted (to divert blood to the brain and muscles). Almost all the stressors we encounter in our day-to-day affairs are cognitive rather than physical, but unfortunately, our systems behave as though we are in immediate danger. The body reacts to our stressful situation by releasing cortisol (and other catecholamines) to provide us with the resources needed to cope with the threat. The stress response increases our chances of surviving physical danger; we either fight or flee, and then the body returns to normal biochemical levels.

But most stress, especially job-related stress, doesn't go away after our bodies have geared up to respond; stressful events are generally continuous and ongoing. Chronic stress can result in a host of circulatory, immune system, and digestive disorders, as anyone with an ulcer can verify; prolonged exposure to stress hormones has been linked to high blood pressure, coronary heart disease, and perhaps even cancer. And if our lives are filled with too much stress, the chronic high cortisol levels we experience can result in the destruction of neurons associated with learning and memory (Vincent, 1990) and a loss of the ability to recognize the important elements of recollections retrieved from memory (Gazzaniga, 1988). In much the same way that fatigue and exhaustion make the body susceptible to viral infection, stress kills brain cells by making them more vulnerable to damage from other causes. Similarly, conditions such as schizophrenia and Parkinson's disease are associated with an imbalance in hormonal levels, as are low self-esteem, recklessness, and aggression (Sylwester, 1995). As stress levels increase, our decision-making abilities begin to suffer.

Our body's response to our environment can lead to positive physiological reactions as well as negative. Another class of peptides released by the sympathetic nervous system, the endorphins, can modulate our emotions by reducing intense pain and increasing our feelings of happiness (Sylwester, 1995). Vigorous exercise and positive social contact with others have been found to elevate endorphin levels with a corresponding increase in feelings of joy and euphoria (Levinthal, 1988). And positive mood states such as happiness have been found to influence the way employees perceive and react to work situations (Williams & T. S. Wong, 1999) and how managers respond to risk (Williams & Y. Wong, 1999). Biochemical responses generated by the brain's interpretation of events can influence the way we make decisions. The chemical neurotransmitters released by our reaction to environmental stimulation convey information to different parts of the brain, as well as moderating our emotional responses and subsequent decision-making abilities.

The human brain is divided into two hemispheres that work in unison to help us interpret and react to the world around us. Each hemisphere consists of four lobes (see Figure 2.1): the *temporal lobe,* which processes

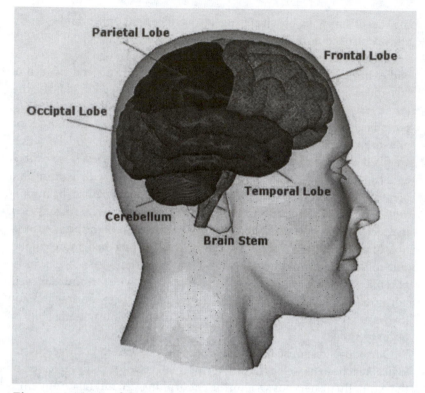

Figure 2.1. Map of the Human Brain

sensory input like hearing and speech and store memories; the *occipital lobe,* which processes what we see; the *parietal lobe,* which handles touch and motor control; and the *frontal lobe,* which deals with critical thinking, planning, and problem solving (Sylwester, 1995). The frontal lobe is believed to house our problem-solving, memory, initiation, judgment, and impulse-control behavior and is responsible for planning our responses to situations, initiating actions, and setting the standards for our social interactions (Kolb & Milner, 1981). The capacity of our frontal lobe to perform critical thinking and problem solving is much greater than what we normally use on a day-to-day basis. Survival generally doesn't depend on the brain to work at full capacity. Our minds hold the surplus capacity in reserve for emergencies and crises, in much the same way that your car doesn't use all the horsepower under the hood until it's needed to pass a slow-moving semitrailer. Many of the activities we enjoy in our spare time, such as games and puzzles, help develop and maintain the decision-making and problem-solving processes we underuse most of the time. When we are confronted with a personal or business problem, our interest and involvement in mind exercises tend to decrease to allow all the resources of our frontal lobe to address our concerns.

Our vastly superior human brain is able to recognize and address uncertainties, abstractions, patterns, and changes rapidly. Almost all of the problems and difficulties we confront require us to create a quick and general response rather than a thorough, complete analysis filled with accuracy. Most of the time, this rapid characterization scheme, which we call common sense or intuition, is perfectly adequate to meet our needs and resolve our problems. The frontal lobe, this "thinking essence" of what we are, serves to regulate, monitor, and control our emotional reactions. This area of the brain allows us to override and constrain the automatic behaviors arising from the rest of the cortex, to stop our impulsive desire to do something destructive or wrong. The prefrontal cortex allows us to plan and rehearse our actions in anticipation of how things might play out in the real world, and this mental ability to predict future events is the primary aspect of the human brain that sets us apart from the lesser animals (Sylwester, 1995).

The brain has adapted to the overflow of sensory stimulation constantly bombarding it by using emotion to draw attention to what is truly important. Emotions are the quick and general reaction to our current situation that focuses our attention so our neural pathways can concentrate on the elements we believe are relevant while the rest of the brain's systems ignore or simply observe the other things going on around us. This emotional/attentional duality is exceedingly quick and extremely powerful. As mentioned earlier, humans are much more likely to survive if they overreact rather than underreact to potential danger; it is better to run away unnecessarily many times and live than to analyze a threat so thoroughly that the decision maker dies well informed. Emotions are the driving force behind our attention, and attention determines what we learn and remember and how we act (Vincent, 1990).

Research has demonstrated that when the frontal lobe is damaged, problem-solving and thinking skills are drastically impaired. For example, people with even slight frontal lobe lesions have great difficulty planning a sequence of complex movements such as making coffee, are unable to persist when trying to focus on a single thought, and cannot focus on tasks they are performing due to a lack of attention span (Kolb & Milner, 1981). The frontal lobes are what enable us to monitor and override our emotional responses and redirect attention to what we think rather than what we feel. But if this part of our mind is damaged or if the emotional response is strong enough to overwhelm our attempts to rein in our impulsive reaction, then our emotions reign supreme and dictate what we decide to do.

We all recognize when people are experiencing extreme emotional states. We clench our fists, cry, gesture abruptly, show flushed faces, or possibly display an emotional outburst. The part of the brain that regulates these responses is a structure called the hypothalamus located near the brain stem. This segment of the brain houses our emotional gateway and is believed to be one of the most primitive and basic components of the mind. It is highly integrated with the autonomic nervous system, the part of our body that controls our heart rate, breathing, and related automatic responses. The hypothalamus triggers our bodily reply to the environment around us by releasing chemicals into our system as well as initiating other physiological responses. The subsequent emotional response, whether negative or positive, directs the brain to focus attention on important aspects of the environment that are causing the sensations we are experiencing. The hypothalamus, through emotional regulation, is telling the brain what is important and where attention needs to be directed.

Analysis of the neural connections within the brain have shown that far more neural fibers project from the brain's emotional center into the rational and logical frontal section than vice versa (LeDoux, 1994). In other words, emotion can overwhelm our logical processes. Even when we restrain our emotional reaction with cool-headed rationality, our underlying feelings are rarely altered. We still feel the same way, even though we may not have responded in the impulsive manner we desired. If the situation is sufficiently powerful, our sympathetic nervous system triggers an immediate defensive or aggressive reaction, activating the fight-or-flight response. This emotional reaction is often so fast that we are barely conscious of it at the rational level. Although the brain may regret our impulsive backlash when scrutinized later by our more objective thought processes, our general makeup is that it's better to be safe and overreact (by becoming emotional) than to be sorry and perform a detailed analysis (by remaining level-headed).

Emotions can fall anywhere along the full spectrum of possibilities, from relatively weak to overpowering. Stronger emotional responses tend to develop from stronger situations, like unexpected loud noises or a potential source of immediate danger. However, a sequence or buildup of situations can eventually push us over the threshold, and a seemingly minor or trivial event can trigger an emotional outburst. To the extent decision makers are able to recognize slowly developing trends, the rational mind can intervene in a timely manner and avert negative outcomes. When emotions and drive states are relatively weak, our rational frontal lobes have no trouble overriding minor impulsive desires to do what is in our best interests. However, as these conditions become stronger, our rational control becomes strained, and we can give in to our immediate wants. And when these states are strong enough, they can overpower any attempt at rationality. For example, if you feel a little sleepy when the alarm goes off in the morning, you might impulsively make a poor long-term decision and turn off the alarm for more sleep even though it is likely you will suffer the consequences of being late for work. You consciously made a decision, even though it was the wrong one. However, if the sleepy feelings you are experiencing are strong enough to make you fall asleep while driving, your decision process has been overridden by physiological factors. We would never consciously decide to go to sleep while driving, but our body makes the decision for us. Similarly, a strong enough emotional reaction such as intense fear or anger can submerge any attempts of the mind to maintain control and act rationally (Loewenstein, 1996).

Our emotional side exists—it's part of what makes us human. Although emotions can be controlled and constrained, they cannot be learned (at least, not in the same way we generally acquire knowledge), and they are very difficult to change. The trick is to know when and how to use our rational thinking self to constrain our emotions and when to allow ourselves the freedom to experience emotions to the fullest.

Our emotions direct attention. Due to the overwhelming complexity of the world around us, it is impossible for us to pay attention to everything. Emotions are triggered by sudden, possibly threatening events, and these changes signal our minds to perk up and do something. The amount of contrast or the intensity of the information received by the mind determines the strength of the message (which is why advertisers use bright lights and loud noises to make us notice). Our perception is geared toward recognizing high-contrast changes; the greater the informational contrast, the more attention we pay to the source. Our initial response is emotional, and the brain's attentional processing determines if a rapid response is necessary. The body's limbic system, the speedy monitoring system that triggers the fight-or-flight reaction, can override rational thought, and we find ourselves following our feelings. The slower frontal cortex mechanism plays an important role in attention processing by allowing us to focus and control our active attention, effectively directing our concentration. The frontal lobes shift our conscious attention and access our memories to see how the current event relates to previous experience. We can all recollect attentively listening to a discussion only to have an unexpected memory suddenly pop into our heads. When we are paying attention, our short-term memory filters what we experience and draws on long-term memory to add relevance and meaning to the experience.

The mind's primary waking function is focusing our attention on whatever is currently important to us. Even when we try to pay attention, we are often sidetracked by additional mental activity and lose our focus. If you've ever missed the exit you wanted to take on the highway because your thoughts wandered or if you suddenly realized that someone asked you a question and you can't remember hearing them speak, then you've experienced how attention can be diverted and go astray. Short-term memory allows us to retain a relatively small number of items to consider, generally about seven bits or chunks of information at a time (Miller, 1956); the phone number you just looked up and are trying to recall and dial often stretches the short-term memory to its limits. This small buffer of working memory allows us to gauge the importance of incoming information, directing our attention quickly and rapidly toward what we perceive. The short-term nature of our attention span is one reason why we have difficulty maintaining our concentration and accuracy when performing long, tedious, and solitary tasks. This disparity between what our senses can register and what our minds can process means that we focus our attention on (and remember) what is most important to us.

The chemicals regulated by the body's nervous system appear to direct this attentional process (Hobson, 1994). For example, neurotransmitter molecules rise sharply in many people around sunrise so we stop sleeping and wake up, and they tend to reach their lowest levels around midnight so we become drowsy and begin to doze. Further demonstration of the body's ability to focus our attention through biochemistry comes from studies involving attention deficit disorder (ADD; Sylwester, 1995). Stimulants that increase both the availability and activity of neurotransmitters often improve the ability of those afflicted with ADD to concentrate and pay attention. Furthermore, a range of uncontrollable behaviors driven by chemicals released in the brain can be moderated by chemical intervention. For example, many neurophysiological based behavior disorders such as compulsions and addictions can be moderated by drugs such as fluoxetine (Loewenstein, 1996), indicating that some decisions we make that are likely to be contrary to our own self-interests can be improved by controlling the physiological impact emotions have on our thinking processes. Science has shown that information processing and decision making are powered by attention, neurotransmitters influence human attention, and emotions trigger the neural response that regulates neurotransmitter activity.

When solving problems, things that are novel, high-contrast, unusual, or emotional seize our attention. The human brain is geared toward allowing emotions to drive our attention so we can quickly determine if a situation is important and potentially threatening. Emotions compel us to act quickly. Any decision confronting us that is perceived as stressful or exciting is likely to trigger a bodily reaction that may result in an inappropriate response. A critical project has a fast-approaching deadline, and we experience a great amount of stress. The chemicals released by our stressful situation make us feel that something is wrong, but then we focus intensely on a trivial or unimportant task rather than coping with the issue at hand. We feel the need to do something, but we end up doing the wrong thing.

Once emotions have been triggered by what we are experiencing, we often allow them to guide the decision-making process and generate outcomes that are contrary to our own self-interests. Immediately experienced emotional factors have a disproportionate influence on our thinking by focusing attention toward the cause of our feelings (Loewenstein, 1996). When we are overcome by "the heat of the moment," we sometimes make decisions that in retrospect we regret or even cannot understand. Unwanted pregnancy and sexually transmitted diseases, for example, can occur because whatever decisions we made about abstaining or using contraception before the fact (when we are cool and rational) are washed away at the actual moment of the decision (when we are impulsive and emotional). A more extreme example would be addicts, who know full well that their decision to indulge in their addiction goes against their long-term well-being but who succumb to their emotional drive for the momentary high they desire or act to avoid the negative feelings associated with withdrawal (Loewenstein, 1996). When heightened emotional drive states like hunger or anger have been triggered, we find it difficult not to satisfy the immediate cravings that direct our attention and related thinking patterns in favor of what might be best for us overall. The biblical character Esau sold his birthright for a bowl of stew; people have confessed to false crimes under the discomfort of interrogation; and life savings have been lost to con men who activate immediate greed. When we say "I don't know what got into me" or "I must have been crazy when I ... " we are remembering how our emotional reaction to the situation had an undue influence on the way we made our decisions. At times like these, our emotional primitive component has controlled the decision-making process rather than the rational planner that strives to maximize our long-term benefit.

The brain has the capability of overriding our impulsive, emotionally laden desires by manipulating our attention and focusing on what is truly important about the problems facing us. Automatic behaviors arising from our emotions can be controlled and regulated by the planning part of the mind, and our frontal cortex enables us to redirect attention to where it needs to be focused. Emotions driven by chemical reactions to our environment turn our attention to what the body thinks is important. Decision makers need to be aware of how their feelings may be influencing their decisional processes. For example, asking the question "Why do I feel this way?" often uncovers the underlying emotional context driving our need to respond. Attention is dictated by the emotional and contrasting elements of our problems, and we need to make a conscious effort to control what we believe is important in making a decision rather than allowing our natural biochemical response unwanted authority in our thinking patterns. Emotion caused by an unconscious biochemical chain of events within the body drives attention, and attention influences decision accuracy. Once we understand how biological factors direct how we *want* to decide, then we are better able to use rational means to shape how we *should* decide.

SUMMARY AND REVIEW

Biological factors influence how we make decisions. Chemical information is passed along by neurotransmitters, and these chemicals trigger our emotional reaction to what we perceive. People possess an amazingly complex and powerful brain that houses our thinking, planning, and judgmental abilities, and it is our frontal lobe that allows us to control and constrain the body's primitive and immediate emotional reactions. Humans are built to use emotions to direct their attention toward environmental events the mind believes might be important. The stronger our emotional reaction to what we are experiencing, the more likely our cool and careful rationality will be overwhelmed by the desire to do something that addresses our immediate desires but goes against our long-term interests. The frontal lobes contain our impulse control center and critical thinking ability. If we allow this rational part of the mind to take control and direct attention toward relevant, rather than emotional aspects of the event we are experiencing, we are able to rein in our impulsive reaction and allow a more thoughtful and reasoned response.

3 | Why We Don't Decide As We Should

The Influence of Want

Y ou find a wallet filled with money on an empty street. You are offered a second piece of rich and tasty dessert after a filling meal. A coworker interrupts you to raise a silly and unimportant issue at a staff meeting, wasting everyone's time. We all know what we *should* do in situations like these, but what do we *want* to do? A problem every decision maker faces is focusing energy and resources thinking about what should be done rather than what we might want to do. When confronted with a problem, our immediate impulse is to do something to address the frustration we feel, rather than restraining our emotions to reflect on what is best in the long run. This Jekyll-and-Hyde battle between the *want* and *should* self has major implications on how decisions are made (Bazerman, Tenbrunsel, & Wade-Benzoni, 1998). As outlined in Chapter 2, the immediacy of the want we feel results from biochemical processes triggered by the body's response to the events we experience.

Many of the decisions we face bring about a compulsive desire to act emotionally and impulsively. You decide to take a job you want rather than the job you believe you ought to have. Rather than deciding to buy the healthier, safer, or cheaper item you know you should get, you purchase the product you want instead. You berate and dismiss as immature two coworkers who come to you with a petty conflict rather than listening calmly to both sides and helping to resolve the issue. You can likely recall several regrettable episodes where you wish you had used reasoned response rather than taking a shortsighted and hotheaded approach. We all know we should maximize our long-term interests, but we often act contrary to what we believe is best by deciding to maximize our short-run gain instead. To understand this inconsistency, we must realize that the rational, level-headed, and thoughtful self who plans what we should do is often vetoed and controlled by an impulsive, emotional, and hotheaded side dictating what we want to do (Thaler, 1980).

Researchers have suggested that decision makers alter the way they perceive a problem when considering an immediate decision in contrast to a decision in the future (Ainslie, 1992; Loewenstein, 1996). Specifically, our physiology is geared such that when we are faced with immediate problems, our impulses and emotions hold more influence, whereas our thoughtful and levelheaded side dominates when we face long-term problems (Bazerman et al., 1998). When contemplating decisions regarding distant outcomes, we tend to be very reflective, rational, and stable. However, as the moment of the decision approaches, our moods, compulsions, and desires exert more influence on our thought processes. We often favor a decision that grants us immediate benefit, forgoing a future alternative that provides even greater benefit (Walsh, 1996). Our emotions indicate importance, and our attention has been focused: The want side of our decisional processes is driven by physiological chemical reactions brought about by our emotional interpretation of the immediate event. The result of this process is that our decision making suffers as our feelings deteriorate. Our ability to control and regulate our emotions and impulses appears to diminish as our emotional distress increases (Tice, Bratslavsky, & Baumeister, 2001). Indications are that when people feel upset, they are more likely to indulge immediate impulses by giving in to their wants in an attempt to make themselves feel better.

Laws in many states are geared toward protecting consumers from this decisional phenomenon. For example, most states allow a period of revocability (usually about 3 days) to allow purchasers of high-priced items such as condominium timesharing or automobiles to reflect on the new acquisition and to cancel ill-advised contracts. Most of us recognize that high-pressure sales pitches focus on the desirable aspects of these types of purchases in an attempt to overwhelm us with vivid or seemingly more salient features of the product (Tversky & Kahneman, 1974). Our rational side is able to exert itself again only when we are removed from the source of the biasing information. In fact, the psychological tactics of con artists, interrogators, and cults are based on the power of immediate wants and desires to drown the long-term self-interest needs of would-be victims. Similarly, lawyers taking depositions often use the initial stages to acquire background facts and only seek potentially damaging information after witnesses show signs of fatigue, loss of concentration, or a willingness to concede points in an attempt to end uncomfortable questioning (Loewenstein, 1996). As emotional distress rises, people often give in to short-term actions in an attempt to improve their current mood state, although their impulsive behaviors may be detrimental to their own long-term interests (Tice et al., 2001).

If we recognize that we are susceptible to undue impulsive influence when making immediate decisions, what can we do to ensure that our decisions are less emotional and more rational? Researchers in the area of self-control have suggested that decision makers are better able to constrain the actions of the hotheaded doer versus the thoughtful planner by applying control techniques. For example, decision makers might establish specific decisional rules ("If I feel angry, I will always sleep on it before I make a decision") or alter incentives ("I'll treat myself to something enjoyable if I don't make snap decisions" or "I'll withhold something enjoyable if I make a snap decision") to control their impulsive natures (Thaler & Shefrin, 1981). Although these methods are likely to have some success, a convincing stream of research suggests that a simple tool the decision maker can apply to minimize the impact of emotional impulse is considering more options (Bazerman et al., 1998), a prescription emphasized in the rational decision process.

Many of our decisions are perceived by us to be one concrete option at a time (Beach, 1990). Every decision can be characterized as an either/or situation: Either accept an option or reject it. Therefore, when we consider a job offer, we might look at it as yes or no, do we take it or do we refuse it? When a decision is framed as accept or reject, our impulsive side is likely to have more influence in the decision. We tend to place greater weight on what we want to do rather than what we should do. However, a decision framed with more options restrains our compulsive nature by forcing us to be more thoughtful by considering the additional alternatives. A decision framed as "Do I accept or reject this job offer?" is more likely to lead us to focus on the emotional aspects of the job that meet perceived wants ("The new job gets me away from my overbearing boss"). Framing the decision with more options ("Do I accept the offer, reject the job offer, attempt to improve the terms of the offer by requesting more money, or consider a different work assignment removing me from the overbearing presence of my current supervisor?") allows the decision maker to minimize the emotional appeal of an either/or viewpoint and to apply a more reasoned and thoughtful approach by considering longer term outcomes.

Studies involving job offers (Bazerman, Schroth, Pradhan, Diekmann, & Tenbrunsel, 1994), marketing decisions (Nowlis & Simonson, 1997), and political preferences (Lowenthal, 1993) have indicated that decision makers tend to be more impulsive and emotional when considering single options and more rational and reasoned when considering multiple options. This line of research has suggested that desirable aspects appear more vivid to our emotional side when we consider single-option outcomes, whereas desires decrease in urgency and importance as we consider more possibilities (Bazerman et al., 1998; Ritov & Kahneman, 1997). Furthermore, if we don't actively seek additional options to consider, we may believe that the single option is the only one available, allowing our impulsive want side undue influence over the decision (Beach, 1990). We are much more likely to serve our short-term interests and act impulsively when we allow ourselves to see decisions as a single option. On the other hand, we appear to be more likely to address our long-term well-being by being more thoughtful and reasoned when we believe that multiple options are open to us.

It is important to recognize the power exercised by our impulsive side. People caught in the grip of a compulsive behavior often characterize themselves as possessing a dual personality: "I knew I shouldn't do it, but I just couldn't help myself." You are on a diet and know you shouldn't eat chocolate, but you snack on a candy bar anyway. You tell yourself that you won't allow an annoying coworker to irritate you, but you have an argument with him the very next time you see him. You say you won't give a likable subordinate a merit raise because of poor work performance but find your resolve has vanished when she smiles at you and asks how much her bonus will be. Emotional responses can suddenly overwhelm us, washing away all our carefully thought out plans. The biochemical response triggered by the temptation of the moment and the possibility of immediate satisfaction or the avoidance of a distasteful negative outcome can have a tremendous impact on the decision we are about to make. As we become emotionally distraught, we tend to indulge our impulses in hopes that giving in will bring pleasure that may improve our mood and banish our feelings of distress (Tice et al., 2001).

An example of how our present feelings can reverse our previous decisional commitments comes from a study of pregnant women before and during childbirth (Christensen-Szalanski, 1984). When asked ahead of time, most pregnant women decide against the use of anesthesia during childbirth, presumably because they believe a more natural labor is healthier for the child. However, once these same women have begun labor and are currently experiencing pain, the majority reverse their initial decision and request anesthesia. Interestingly, in this study, decision reversal was equally likely regardless of the number of previous births the mother had experienced—even those who had realistic expectations about their labor pains made predecisions to avoid anesthesia and then changed their minds. The strength of our current wants exerts more influence at the time of the event and can alter our previous intentions.

If our decision-making attention is leading us in a particular direction, we should be aware of the reasons behind our impulse. Strong emotions have been triggered by the body's self-protection mechanism, and the cause of these underlying feelings needs to be considered. Stronger emotions such as anger and fear often spur us to make snap judgments. A quick decision isn't necessarily an incorrect one—simplified decision rules can work quite well. People often find themselves deciding intuitively and instinctively when faced with a situation that "just doesn't feel right" or one that "feels like the right thing to do" (Dunegan, 1995). The quality of our decision benefits if the source of our feelings can be recognized and we can determine if our emotions are having a disproportionate influence on our thinking. Our impulsive side, stoked by the degree of our emotional involvement, wants us to decide in its favor for a reason. Before we act, we must uncover the source of our feelings. To the extent possible, outcomes that address and at least partially satisfy the desires of our impulsive side should be realistically considered; otherwise, our feelings can potentially overrule our attempts at rational control (Bazerman et al., 1998; Thaler & Shefrin, 1981). For example, a supervisor who has decided that an employee does not merit a pay raise due to unsatisfactory work performance (the *should* decision) and who considers deciding in favor of granting a salary increase when confronted by the subordinate (the *want* decision) must recognize the underlying cause behind the conflicting decisions. It is possible that the intuitive impulse senses that although the employee's work performance is admittedly poor, her willingness to assist others and the optimism she brings to the workplace counterbalance the established evaluation criteria to some degree. Or the decision may simply flow from a desire to avoid a negative reaction from the employee when she is informed that no pay raise is forthcoming. In either case, the decision maker should root out the underlying source of the discomfort and recognize it as a potential influence in the decision-making process. The possibility of giving in to compulsion must be acknowledged and understood, not only because our impulses can hijack our rational intentions, but also because our feelings have likely found something our thoughtful planning side has either overlooked or analyzed incorrectly (Loewenstein, 1996). So when the decision we arrive at in the cool light of day (such as to abstain from sex) has a realistic chance of being overturned during the heat of the moment, then we need to take our emotional side very seriously and attempt to devise a compromise both sides can live with rather than deciding impulsively to do something that is contrary to our own best interests.

SUMMARY AND REVIEW

Often, we must decide between what we want to do and what we should do. The *want* side of our human nature is the impulsive, emotional, and hotheaded doer, whereas our *should* side is the rational, level-headed, and thoughtful planner. Our should side generally makes rational decisions that are in our best long-term interests, but it is the want side that can take control of our thinking processes at the time of the actual decision and override all our carefully laid out plans. By forcing ourselves to consider more options during decision making, we decrease the likelihood that our impulsive nature will be able to exert undue influence. Furthermore, if a strong possibility exists that our emotional nature will hijack the decision process at the time of the event, we need to take our wants seriously and attempt to address these intuitive concerns to minimize the chances of satisfying our immediate needs while forgoing our future interests.

4 | Judgmental Biases
Influencing Decisions

M ost of our judgments result from decisional shortcuts we use to generate solutions that are good enough most of the time. Several job applicants have impressive résumés, but we hire based on the impressions we derive from face-to-face interviews. Two subordinates come to us with a personal conflict, but we quickly decide to do nothing because this type of problem usually resolves itself if we take a hands-off approach. When selecting among a variety of possible projects to fund, we choose the one with the fastest payback rate. Decisional shortcuts that achieve reasonably good outcomes enable us to save time and effort. However, decision makers are susceptible to a number of judgmental biases that systematically lead to predictable inconsistencies and decisional errors (Nisbett & Ross, 1980). Because these shortcuts can lead us astray, we need to be aware of how potential biasing can have a predictable impact on our decisions.

SELECTIVE PERCEPTION

Take a look at the following picture (Figure 4.1) and come up with some words that describe the woman you see. Did you decide that she was young or old? Pretty or unattractive? Rich or poor? Most people classify

Figure 4.1. Woman A

the woman in this picture as young, pretty, and wealthy. Now look at the following picture (Figure 4.2) and see if you would use the same words to describe the woman shown. Most likely you would still agree that she is relatively young, attractive, and rich.

However, people who are initially shown the woman in Figure 4.3 and then are asked to describe the woman in Figure 4.2 almost always say she is old, unattractive, and poor, words describing the opposite of what others see in the very same picture. When shown either the relatively unambiguous picture of the young or old woman (Figures 4.1 and 4.3) first and then the composite picture (Figure 4.2), *selective perception* has been triggered. Exposure to either picture draws our attention to seek out cues in the following picture that support what we expect to see, and our thinking processes willingly oblige by confirming that the second picture lives up to our expectations.

We are constantly bombarded with so much sensory information that it is impossible for us to pay attention to everything. Our subconscious mind scans our environment and selects what it deems may be important for us to notice. Even then, people not only see things the way they are, they also tend to see what they expect to see, as well as what they want to see (Plous, 1993). Optical illusions—rooms in which water appears to flow uphill and magic acts—are examples of how our assumptions and expectations influence what we think we see.

When we perceive a situation that looks familiar to us, our past experience often causes us to see the event in terms of what we expect. Our limited span of attention leads us to categorize things by aspects that appear similar to what we already know, and we save time and energy by assuming the current situation is comparable to previous experiences (Bruner & Postman, 1949). We expect, for example, the new hire from a prestigious business school to ask probing and pertinent questions. When this employee speaks up at a staff meeting, his or her comments receive more weight because we anticipate the questions will be more meaningful than those asked by someone else. We expect insightful comments, so we believe remarks *must* be more discerning. If we expect the bad guys who wear black to do bad things, it is not surprising to discover that sports teams with black uniforms receive far more penalties than other teams (Frank & Gilovich, 1988). And if police officers expect that red cars are more likely to speed, then we begin to understand why drivers of red auto-

Figure 4.2. Woman B

mobiles get a higher number of traffic violations than those who drive cars of other colors.

We not only tend to see what we expect, but we are also susceptible to seeing things the way we want them to be (Cowan, 1986). For example, most people believe they are above average in intelligence (Wylie, 1979) as well as highly skilled drivers (Svenson, 1981), because we want to believe flattering things about ourselves. This "Lake Wobegon Effect" results in a perception that "the women are strong, the men are good-looking, and all the children are above average" ("Word Watch," 1989). When considering information, we require different kinds and amounts of evidence if the facts we have gathered fail to support our preferences. People who are heavily committed to a given position allow the weight of their beliefs to influence how a situation is perceived. When proponents of opposite sides of an issue are asked how an event associated with their stance is perceived, they tend to develop different and contradictory perceptions (Vallone, Ross, & Lepper, 1985). Employees who are strongly in favor of one side of a controversial work issue will actually perceive a meeting called to discuss possible options in a fundamentally different way than employees in the opposite camp.

We are extremely willing to take the credit for our successes, and we blame our failures on external circumstances beyond our control (Nisbett & Ross, 1980). When sports teams win, it is because of their hard work and talent. When they lose, it is due to bad officiating, weather conditions, lack of fan support, and so on. And students who perform well on a test do so because they understand the material, are knowledgeable, or possibly because they are gifted test-takers. However, those who perform poorly on the very same test accuse the professor of testing uncovered material, offering poorly worded questions, or applying unfair grading practices. We perceive internal causes for desirable outcomes and external interference for unfavorable consequences.

ISN'T IT FUNNY

When the other fellow takes a long time to do something, he's slow, but when I take a long time to do something, I'm thorough.

When the other fellow doesn't do it, he's too lazy, but when I don't do it, I'm too busy.

Figure 4.3. Woman C

When the other fellow goes ahead and does something without being told, he's overstepping his bounds, but when I go ahead and do something without being told, that's initiative.

When the other fellow states his side of a question strongly, he's bullheaded, but when I state my side strongly, I'm being firm.

When the other fellow overlooks a few of the rules of etiquette, he's rude, but I'm original.

When the other fellow does something that pleases the boss, he's polishing the brass, but when I do it, that's cooperation.

When the other fellow gets ahead, he sure had the lucky breaks, but when I succeed, well, that's hard work!

—Anonymous

The strength of our emotional attachment to our beliefs creates a filter that screens all comments and actions in light of how they relate to our position. Selective perception can cause two employees holding contrary positions at a meeting to perceive the same action (such as a comment by the boss) as unfairly biased and hostile to the side they advocate. Disagreements are not just differences of opinion or attitude but actual differences in how people see the event (Plous, 1993). When assessing a problem, the stance we take toward an issue, especially a controversial one, may be based on our selective screening of information. Facts that appear to be opposed to our beliefs are not ignored, but rather we hold them to a higher level of scrutiny than when we are not so heavily committed to a particular way of thinking. The content of the contradictory information is either "massaged" to be consistent with our expectations, or we determine it is flawed, hopelessly deficient, and of little value (Gilovich, 1993).

To cope with potential selection effects, we need to ask ourselves: Would an impartial outsider also view the situation in the same way? If not, are we justified to maintain our position? Are we allowing our emotions to filter information and influence our thought processes? For example, are we seeking information to confirm our beliefs (which can almost always be found) rather than trying to find facts that disconfirm what we expect? Do our expectations predispose us to lean in a given direction? For example, are we consulting sources of information that are predisposed to our way of thinking (which will invariably lead us to believe our expectations were correct)? Has our perception of the problem altered once information became available? Also, an active attempt to see the situation from as many different perspectives as possible gives us a broader and more realistic representation of what we are perceiving. For positions we do not wish to believe, are we applying a different standard of acceptability? Are we framing unpalatable decisions in such a way that the evidence must be overwhelming to convince us to change our mind, while we need only mild support to persuade us of the correctness of positions we find more favorable?

IMPRESSION EFFECTS

The timing of when we are exposed to and recall aspects of the problems we face can influence our judgment. A *primacy effect* occurs when initial impressions are believed to be more relevant and important in rendering a decision than later impressions. Consistent evidence has been found to indicate that first impressions often are lasting ones (Asch, 1946), demonstrating that the sage advice mothers give their children "to be sure and make a good first impression" has merit. You remain impressed by the qualifications of your newly hired subordinate (perhaps he graduated cum laude from a top-notch business school) in spite of dismal work performance and a tendency toward tardiness. You've positively judged the employee, and it generally requires fairly persuasive evidence to overturn what was initially believed to be true. We have all been introduced to strangers and had a first response that something just wasn't quite right about them, or we might be struck with an immediate feeling of liking and attraction toward them. Our first impressions are intuitive. Our always working subconscious processes have detected something about the person that triggers an emotional reaction resulting in feelings of like or dislike. Many times, our instinctive reaction is justified—when we are informed that people who made a bad first impression have done something negative, we respond by nodding wisely and saying we never did feel quite right about them in the first place. However, first impressions can also be misleading. Some attributes (such as attractiveness or high energy levels) often lead us to believe that people possessing such desirable qualities must have other positive dimensions as well (Dion, Berscheid, & Walster, 1972). In addition, it is likely that negative primacy effects carry more weight than positive ones (Nisbett & Smith, 1989). If we've formed a negative impression of someone, we tend to avoid that person, and the opportunity rarely arises for our beliefs to be changed.

The primacy effect can occur when decision makers evaluate situations as well as people. When we are exposed to opposite sides of a controversial issue, the first presentation can carry more weight than subsequent presentations (Plous, 1993). However, sometimes, it is the most recent incident that is perceived as being more important. This pattern of recalling the last event more clearly and believing it to be more important than previous events is known as the *recency effect.* A supervisor is compiling performance appraisals for the entire department. When she tries to recall the performance of a particular employee, she remembers that the last time she walked by his desk, he was busily working on an assigned project. Her most recent recollection carries more weight in her evaluation of his performance than the not-so-vivid memories of the times she walked by his desk and he was nowhere to be found. Because the event is more vivid and more readily recalled from memory, it evokes a stronger emotional response on our decision processes (Tversky & Kahneman, 1973). The recency effect can have a negative impact as well. The supervisor recalls that an employee had to be reprimanded just yesterday, an event that overshadows the worker's previous year of high levels of trouble-free work performance. All of us are intuitively aware of the possible impact of the recency effect on decision making. Students are especially friendly to their professors just before finals week, hoping to influence upcoming grades. Workers are extremely nice and noticeably busy right before merit raises are to be assigned, anticipating that the boss will remember them more favorably at decision time. Furthermore, studies demonstrate that when we are in a particular mood (either positive or negative), we are more likely to remember events that are similar to our current state (Wright & Bower, 1992). So when we feel good, we find it easier to remember situations where we also felt good, and when we are feeling bad, we are more likely to recall similar times when we were also in a bad mood.

When primacy and recency effects come into play at the same time, the one that has the greatest impact on decision making depends on the situation. As an example, would it be preferential to be the first speaker in a staff debate or the last? Regardless of whether your stance is pro or con (whether you are for or against the issue under discussion), studies indicate that primacy and recency don't sway our decisions much if a judgment is required immediately after both sides have finished presenting (Miller & Campbell, 1959). However, if the decision will be delayed by as much as a week, primacy carries more weight—the side presenting first is likely to have more influence on the subsequent decision. On the other hand, if the second side to the issue isn't communicated until a later date (perhaps at the next staff meeting), recency carries more weight—the side presenting last is likely to have more influence on the judgment. To benefit from possible primacy or recency effects, you should choose to present your side of an issue first if the matter won't be decided until later. However, you should choose to present last if a period of time separates the discussion of the two sides and a decision will be reached right after hearing the second position.

Salespeople often use a similar procedure when trying to persuade us to purchase their products. In an attempt to appear fair, some salespeople list the favorable or pro aspects of the product they are pitching followed by a (usually much shorter) list of possible negatives or con aspects. When the pros and cons are presented back to back in this fashion and then the would-be buyer is asked to make an immediate buying decision, the seller is using the power of the primacy effect to prime the consumer's favorable response pattern. If the buyer postpones judgment and takes additional time to consider the purchase, then the recency effect is more likely to influence the buying decision, and the list of negatives will seem more relevant to the decision process.

The *halo effect* occurs when we believe a single characteristic possessed by someone is associated with a host of other desirable traits. For example, most attractive people are also believed to be smarter (Landy & Sigall, 1974), warm people are seen as sociable and humorous (Kelley, 1950), and intelligent people are rated as better leaders (Thorndike, 1920). In the workplace, if a supervisor believes a subordinate possesses a positive attribute (such as being hard-working), the manager may also believe the worker has additional desirable characteristics, such as punctuality and honesty. As with other perceptual biases, the halo effect may sway our decision making if we allow one condition of a situation to color additional aspects. Many people (like politicians) successfully exploit the halo effect by implying they can accomplish a wide range of outcomes based on one previous accomplishment. The opposite of the halo effect (sometimes called a negative halo or the devil's horns effect) occurs when we attribute a number of additional undesirable traits to someone based on our observance of one negative aspect. For example, people who are untidy in appearance may also be viewed as lazy and untrustworthy. As with other perceptual biases, the halo effect can unconsciously influence our judgments by implying that unsubstantiated attributes also exist.

Impression effects are subtle and can be enduring. Furthermore, impression effects have the tendency to perpetuate themselves. When evaluating résumés for potential new employees, interviewers tend to focus on one or two bits of information and make their initial impressions. When candidates are interviewed, those with favorable first impressions and stronger halo expectations are treated more pleasantly and tapped for confirming information by interviewers, rather than being treated without bias (Dougherty, Turban, & Callender, 1994). Being aware of our susceptibility to their biasing impact and making a conscious effort to be objective in our evaluations are ways we can attempt to reduce impression effects on our decisions.

PRESENTATION EFFECTS

Unbelievable as it may seem, something as simple as how we receive information can influence the decisions we make. *Presentation effects* occur when how we receive information influences how we decide. For example, people decide they have more headaches if asked whether they get headaches *frequently* rather than *occasionally;* movies are believed to be much longer if we are asked how *long* a movie was rather than how *short,* and we gauge people to be of a much greater height when asked to remember how *tall* someone was rather than how *short* (Plous, 1993). We often use an initial value (such as *frequently* or *tall*) as a starting point in our assessments and adjust from that beginning to achieve a final decision (Dawes, 1988). However, many times, our subsequent adjustments from the initial anchor point tend to be insufficient (Slovic & Lichtenstein, 1971).

If you were told that people *who know very little* about the computer industry guess that an Internet Web master (to develop and maintain a company's Web page) should be paid about $40,000 per year, what would your annual salary estimate for this position be? About the same? Slightly more or slightly less? What if the estimate cited above had been $100,000 per year? When presented with a similar problem, most decision makers will give higher salary estimates if given a higher base rate, even when they are informed (as in the example above) that the information they are receiving is relatively meaningless (Tversky & Kahneman, 1974). We tend to latch onto any information we feel may assist our decision making (no matter how inappropriate or misleading). Moreover, how information is presented to us can also influence the way we use it to make decisions. For example, presenting jurors with potential verdicts that start with the harshest and end with the most lenient leads to substantially more severe punishments than considering possibilities in the opposite order (Greenberg, Williams, & O'Brien, 1986). Anchoring occurs frequently in business settings when questions are framed with a figure inserted rather than using unspecified amounts. Asking whether we believe the new project will cost more than $10 million establishes an unintended (possibly) starting point and will almost always result in a different response than if we were asked how much the new project will likely cost without providing the initial figure.

The tendency for decision makers to anchor from an initial starting point can influence our judgment. If we are presented with information suggesting that funding for a project may run as high as $1.5 million and are subsequently asked to decide an appropriate budget, we may allow the anchor to constrain our options by limiting possible amounts to that range. Similarly, when evaluating an employee for a pay increase, we may confine our possibilities to an average salary adjustment, even though the individual may have been severely under- or overpaid in comparison to industry averages; and initial positions in similar negotiations may anchor later decisions (Bazerman, 1990). Or we may allow extraneous information to influence our judgment of something's "true" worth when an anchor causes us to judge the object as either more or less valuable than it actually is. For example, even experts shifted their evaluation of real estate (by an average of $10,000) when presented with one inaccurate fact in a 10-page information packet (Northcraft & Neale, 1987). The limited short-term information-processing capacity of the human mind leads decision makers to focus on the most important aspects of a situation to solve a problem. Research indicates that even outrageously extreme anchors can unknowingly sway our judgments (Quattrone et al., 1984). Although we may instinctively realize that a given base rate should not be allowed to influence our thought processes, it appears that our subconscious mind locks onto information that seems to be relevant, establishing an initial starting point that tends to swing our thinking in the direction of the anchor.

During job interviews, it is common practice for the interviewer to ask prospective hires the salary range they anticipate for the job. Interviewees who offer an amount, especially one that is too low, may allow themselves to fall victim to anchoring. The interviewer is likely to anchor on the given figure and adjust upward or downward only slightly, narrowing the salary range under consideration. Anchoring effects suggest that during the interview process, we are better served by responding with a less concrete answer that allows the salary range to be more flexible. Similarly, when negotiating to buy a used car, the first party to offer a figure is likely to be disadvantaged. An asking or selling price that is lower than the other party would have been willing to pay presents an anchoring point and limits the range of possibilities that might have been considered.

When information becomes an anchor, we adjust insufficiently from that amount when making decisions. This is why persuasive arguments can sometimes be very successful if they present extreme initial views. Often, we are not even aware that an anchor value has been allowed to sway our judgment. Because of their pervasiveness, presentation effects can have a significant impact on business decisions. For example, if we are contemplating major changes and we only consider the "best case" scenario, we are unlikely to generate a realistic expectation about the future. Even though we "tone down" our projections, it is still very likely that our impressions are biased. Generally, it is helpful to come up with multiple possibilities to provide additional anchor values.

To minimize presentation effects, it helps if we are able to recall and consider events that occurred both before and after what readily comes to mind. Increasing the number of items under consideration generally gives us a more accurate picture of what a person or situation is really like. Furthermore, playing devil's advocate helps to uncover the reasons why we feel as we do. Do we really have justification for believing as we do, or are we allowing key characteristics or events to unduly sway our judgment?

FRAMING EFFECTS

Imagine that you are the general manager of a production company during a major economic recession, which is expected to result in the loss of 900 jobs at your factory. You are presented with the following two proposals:

- Proposal 1 will save 300 jobs.
- Proposal 2 has a one in three chance of saving all 900 jobs, and a two in three chance of saving no jobs.

Which of these two proposals would you choose? Most people, when presented with a problem similar to the one above, tend to try to avoid risk and select Proposal 1 (Tversky & Kahneman, 1981). They prefer the sure thing of saving at least 300 jobs rather than risking the chance of saving no jobs to save all jobs.

How would you respond to the next two proposals?

- Proposal A will result in 600 job losses.
- Proposal B has a one in three chance that no jobs will be lost, and a two in three chance that all jobs will be lost.

Did you change your decision? Notice Proposals 1 and A are numerically equivalent: saving 300 jobs (of the 900 total) is the same thing as losing 600 jobs. Similarly, Proposals 2 and B are the same: a one in three chance of saving all jobs is equal to a two in three chance that all jobs will be lost, and a two in three chance of saving no jobs is the same as a one in three chance of losing all 600 jobs. Most decision makers, when presented with the second set of options, prefer to take the gamble (Proposal B) rather than face the sure prospect of losing 600 jobs. Our final decision is influenced by how we frame the problem because losses loom larger than gains. In the first set of proposals (Proposals 1 and 2), the options are framed in terms of saving jobs. When we evaluate the safety of a sure gain against the possibility of a major loss, our tendency is to embrace the definite good and forgo the possible disaster (as the truism "A bird in the hand is worth two in the bush" would suggest). In the second set of proposals (Proposals A and B), the options are framed in terms of losing jobs. When faced with an unavoidable loss, our tendency is to grasp opportunities that may salvage the situation (Bazerman, 1990). The emotional discomfort we experience from losing jobs is more extreme than the positive feelings we derive from saving the same number of jobs. When presented with decisions involving potential losses, we are more willing to take risks to avoid those losses. And when presented with problems framed to emphasize possible gains, we are more willing to accept the sure thing and tend to shy away from risks (Highhouse & Yuce, 1996).

Consider receiving a B grade for a course. Your instructor offers you the option of either accepting the given grade or flipping a fair coin. If heads occurs, your grade becomes an A, but if the coin shows tails, you get a C. Would you be willing to take the risk? Now consider that the grade you received was a D, and you are offered the opportunity to flip for either a C or an F. Are you more willing to take the risk now? When presented with this scenario, many students are unwilling to take the risk in the first situation because they feel a B is a gain (a good enough grade) and choose not to gamble on the possibility of making things worse. However, most students say they would be willing to risk the coin toss to turn a D (a loss) into a better grade.

Framing effects occur when decision makers tend to avoid risk when problems are framed as gains and seek risk when problems are viewed as losses. The effects of problem framing have been found in other types of decisions as well. For example, when patients are asked to select the form of cancer treatment they prefer, how the information is presented to them influences their decisions. More lung cancer patients select surgery when they are told that they have a "68% chance of living for more than 1 year" rather than when they are told that surgery results in a "32% chance of dying by the end of the year" (Wilson, Kaplan, & Schneiderman, 1987). Similarly, framing can sway our evaluation of an attribute if it is presented to us positively rather than negatively. For example, ground beef is usually labeled as "80% lean" rather than "20% fat" to influence our judgments of health and taste (Levin & Gaeth, 1988), or a shampoo is labeled as containing "1% natural protein" rather than 99% non-protein ingredients. An employee whose attendance is framed in positive terms (for example, the percentage of days present on the job) is likely to be evaluated more favorably than another employee with the exact same rate of absenteeism whose attendance is framed negatively (the percentage of days absent from the job). People have a general tendency to evaluate the same characteristic more positively when given a positive description than when given a negative description (Levin, 1987).

Not only does the framing of our choices influence our decision processes, but the framing of the outcomes of our choices has an impact on how we think as well (Tversky & Kahneman, 1981). Suppose you need a personal calculator for your job. After you enter the store and make your choice, the salesperson informs you that the $20 model you are ready to purchase is on sale at another location for $10. Would you travel to the other store to buy the calculator? Most consumers would (Tversky & Kahneman, 1981). Now, suppose you need a personal computer for your job. After you enter the store and make your choice, the salesperson informs you that the $1,000 model you are ready to purchase is available at another location for $990. Would you travel to the other store to buy the computer? Most consumers would not. In the first situation, most of us perceive the cost difference in terms of percentages: An item that is half off is worth the extra effort. In the second situation, the difference between $1,000 and $990 is seen as insignificant relative to the effort involved; the savings are only a fraction of the overall cost. Objectively, the same $10 difference exists in both cases. Of course, if the absolute amount saved is large enough, regardless of its relative percentage, then consumers are likely to frame the decision in terms of the overall savings (Darke & Freedman, 1993). However, for many judgments, if the decision is framed in terms of relative amount saved, we decide one way. If the decision is framed in absolute terms, we decide differently.

Another example of how outcome framing can affect our judgment is how our point of comparison is established (Bazerman, 1990). Say your uncle died 5 years ago and left you 1,000 shares of stock valued at the time at $100 per share. Since you received your inheritance, the stock price has dropped to $50 per share. Word is out that the company in which you own stock is considering a merger. Analysts estimate a 50-50 probability that the merger will result in an "all or nothing" outcome: Your stock will either regain its value and be worth $100 a share, or the merger will result in complete bankruptcy and your stock will have no value at all. Will you sell your stock today at $50 per share?

Your answer will depend in large part on how you frame the problem. If you believe the stock is worth $100 a share (the original value), then you are more likely to hold onto it rather than accept a guaranteed loss of $50 for each share. However, if you frame the situation as one in which you invested none of your own money in the stock because it was a gift (your reference point is $0 per share because you had nothing before), then you are much more likely to take the guaranteed gain and sell for $50 per share. If we perceive the decision as one of loss, we will tend to be risk seeking (take the gamble), and if we see the choice as one of gain, we will avoid risk (take the sure thing).

If your company is being sued for $100,000 and your lawyers inform you that you have a 50-50 chance of losing in court, will you accept an offer to settle for $50,000? What if your company is suing another firm for $100,000 with a 50-50 chance of losing, and they offer $50,000 to settle out of court. Would you accept? If your answer is different for these two scenarios, then it is likely that your perception as to whether the situation is a gain or a loss is influencing your judgment. We are more likely to bet on the long shot during the last race of the day when we have lost money than when we have previously won, because we view the gamble as a potential means of recovering from our loss. In a similar fashion, if you have worked in your current position for a number of years and receive a job offer with a new firm that offers high risk and high opportunity, would you take it? One factor that will influence our decision is how we perceive our current position in comparison with our expectations of where we think we should be at this stage in our career. If we are satisfied with our progress, it is much more likely that we will believe where we are is a gain and stay with our safe job, not taking the gamble offered by the new position. However, if our current job fails to meet our expectations of where our career should be, then we are much more likely to see our current position as a loss (compared to the point we believe we should be) and take the risk.

What we own is much more valuable to us than what we do not possess. A sizable (sometimes very large) discrepancy exists between what we are willing to pay to acquire something and then what we would require to lose the same item. If you were asked how much you would be willing to pay to have another person clean your place for 4 hours, what is the most you would be willing to pay? Compare that amount with the least you would be willing to accept to clean for someone else for the same 4 hours. It is not uncommon for us to demand from 5 to 20 times as much for our own time compared to what we would be willing to pay others (Bazerman, 1990). We require more for our time because to give it up is considered a loss, but we are unwilling to pay as much to gain additional free time.

Research suggests that decision makers perceive equal situations differently depending on how they are framed (Frisch, 1993). Due to our limited mental capacity, we bias our thinking when we focus on the descriptive elements used to categorize what we see. To prevent our senses from being overwhelmed, what we perceive is condensed, summarized, and recorded by the mind according to what seems to be the most important aspect of the situation. Although we might recognize at an intellectual level that a glass that is half full is the same as one that is half empty, different frames systematically distort how we react to identical situations and how we make decisions.

To combat possible framing effects, it helps if we are able to frame problems in terms of what it is we are trying to accomplish. Looking at a situation from the conclusion backward often allows us to frame our problems more objectively. Also, we should never automatically accept a frame as it is given to us; others who are close to the problem generally look at the problem the same way we do. We should always try to reframe the situation and look for possible risk distortion. Furthermore, if we are able to play devil's advocate and generate reasons why the opposite frame is a viable way to view the problem, we are less likely to become trapped in a one-dimensional understanding of the risks and gains associated with the problem at hand.

ESCALATION OF COMMITMENT EFFECTS

Given the several thousand business decisions made every day, some are bound to be unsuccessful. Rationally, it makes sense that once we recognize that we've made a bad decision, we should take steps to correct the situation by "cutting our losses." However, often, bad solutions are followed by even more ineffective decisions. Investors purchase more and more shares of a company, even though the stock price keeps on declining. Large banks continue to funnel funds into foreign countries whose economies are collapsing in hopes a turnaround will result. Organizers pour large amounts of money into an operation even when it's apparent the event will lose money (Ross & Staw, 1986). The tendency for people to "throw good money after bad" is known as the *escalation of commitment*— decisions that continue to support previously unsuccessful courses of action because too much has been invested to quit (Conlon & Garland, 1993). We often allow "sunk costs" or historical investment of time, resources, and effort that cannot be salvaged to influence future decisions.

We are sometimes forced to make a decision as a result of a previous decision. For example, you personally hired a new employee you believed would be an excellent performer in your department (Bazerman, Beekun, & Schoorman, 1982). However, initial indications are that she isn't going to live up to your expectations, and in fact, she even seems to be having a detrimental effect on her colleagues. Should you terminate her? Perhaps she just needs time to adjust, and after all, you invested a lot of time and money in her selection and training. After more time passes, it still seems as though she isn't working out, but now you have even more invested in her hoped-for success. Should you fire her, or wait and see if things improve? When will you possess enough information to cut your losses? Escalation of commitment explains why rational decision makers would continue to infuse funding and soldiers into wars that are unlikely to end, such as the U.S.-Vietnam conflict, and why superpowers like the United States and Russia would invest so heavily to get ahead in an "unwinnable" nuclear arms race.

What if you've invested a significant amount of money in a project that has spent its budgeted amount but has yet to prove successful. You're faced with two choices: either accept the loss and end the project or infuse more capital into the project in hopes of turning things around. How would you decide? On a more personal level, anyone who has been put on hold while on the telephone faces escalating commitment. Do you hang up and try again later, or do you stay on the line thinking that you've already invested so much time that to give up now would be wasteful? Do you pay for expensive repairs on your car because you have already paid so much for its upkeep, or is it time to look for a new set of wheels? Not surprisingly, when sunk costs are removed from our decision analysis, people tend to make different decisions. For example, people who were informed that $10 million had already been invested in a product 90% completed (a product inferior and more expensive than a newcomer to the market) believed that further money should be invested to complete the project. However, when they were asked whether the project should continue but were given no previous cost information, almost all decision makers decided to end the project (Arkes & Blumer, 1985).

Decision makers willingly escalate their commitment to unsuccessful decisions for a number of reasons. First, failure to support our own previous action openly acknowledges that the initial decision was a mistake, forcing us to "lose face" and reducing our political credibility (Bobocel &

Meyer, 1994). We seek self-justification and desire to look good to our-selves and others by proving that we are indeed rational and competent at resolving problems; therefore, we decide to continue even though all indi-cations are that we should stop. Second, as mentioned under framing ef-fects, the way we frame a problem influences our subsequent decision. The obvious loss of discontinuing a previous course of action biases us to prefer to "take the gamble" in hopes of gains that may be realized if only we persevere long enough (Tversky & Kahneman, 1981). Third, decision makers often believe that persistence is necessary and desirable to weather the storm and get back on course (Northcraft & Wolf, 1984). After all, tra-ditional wisdom insists that "if at first you don't succeed, try, try again," and the future may still prove that our initial decision was correct. And fourth, as the amount of responsibility felt by the decision maker for the original decision rises, the likelihood of escalating commitment increases (Staw, 1976). When we feel personally responsible for making the first de-cision, negative feedback about what we did biases us by limiting our ob-jectivity and changing how we view and evaluate alternatives. So if you are the one who decided to hire a new employee, you are not only less likely to fire her, but you are also more likely to distort your perceptions of her work performance and abilities in her favor (Bazerman et al., 1982).

Commitment escalation can also occur because of our tendency to-ward selective perception (Bazerman, 1990). As discussed previously, we have a tendency to see what we expect to see, seeking information that supports our expectations. So if we were the one responsible for hiring the new employee, we are more likely to focus on information that supports our initial decision and either discount or minimize information dis-confirming our hiring decision. If we were the one responsible for the investment in a questionable enterprise, we are also more likely to be the one who sees the situation in a more positive light than uninvolved ob-servers. Selective perception suggests that we may filter subsequent infor-mation to allow us to maintain our commitment to a freely chosen course of action (Staw, 1976).

Of course, other factors, such as aspects of our personality (Schaubroeck & Williams, 1993), can alter our likelihood to reinvest, but how do we minimize the effects of escalating commitment? Research indicates esca-lating commitment can be minimized if we set limits on the amount of funding available and the degree of our commitment *in advance* (Rubin, 1980). We are not trapped by the temptation of persevering with a failing course of action because we can justify ending our commitment by sticking to our established limit. Auctions are good examples of this phenomenon. People often end up bidding much more than they desired for an item (due to the heat of the moment and the competition involved) if they fail to establish a cutoff point ahead of time to limit possible escalation. To avoid becoming entrapped, we need to explicitly consider the costs of withdrawal before a commitment (such as investing in a long-term venture) is made (Staw & Ross, 1987). Also, to the extent we are able to *diffuse* the responsibility we feel for the initial decision, commitment bias can be lessened (Whyte, 1991). If we can recognize that the failing course of action does not belong to us alone, then we are less likely to attempt to justify the initial decision by continuing in the wrong direction. In most company settings, major investment decisions are made by more than one employee, allowing decision makers to share ownership of a particular course of action and ease the need to feel personally responsible. To avoid commitment escalation, decision makers need to evaluate future costs from the current situation rather than including unrecoverable historic costs.

CATEGORIZATION EFFECTS

Suppose you are introduced to someone and after a short conversation with her, you discover that she is 31 years old, single, outspoken, and very bright. She seems to be deeply concerned with social issues, and you find out that she was once arrested during an antinuclear demonstration. Do you believe that this person is more likely to be (a) a bank teller or (b) a bank teller who is active in the feminist movement? Most people select Alternative b, although Alternative a is the correct response (Tversky & Kahneman, 1982). To see why, decide whether it is more likely that (a) Iraq will invade Iran or (b) Iraq will invade Iran and the United States will take military action. Again, Option a is the correct answer. Notice that in both of these examples, the second response includes the first response as a subset. It is always more likely that a single event will occur rather than the single event in conjunction with another event. In mathematical terms, X alone will always occur more often than X alone + Y. The chance that two uncertain events will happen together is always less than the odds of either happening alone. So it is much more likely that someone will be a bank teller rather than a bank teller *and* a feminist, and it is much more likely that Iraq will invade Iran rather than that Iraq will invade Iran *and* the United States will get involved. However, we believe the co-occurrence alternative is more likely because it appears to be more representative of how we imagine things should be (Plous, 1993). Someone who possesses the characteristics described in the first example is more representative of what we expect a feminist to be like, and we allow that perception to influence our decision. Similarly, one nation invading another would be representative of why the U.S. would become involved in the Middle East, and our choice is influenced by our perceptual bias.

Representativeness, which is when we perceive information as typical (or representative) of the particular category to which it belongs (Kahneman & Tversky, 1973), can lead us to make incorrect assumptions when making decisions. For example, decide if an MBA student who is very interested in the arts and at one time considered a music career is more likely to take a job (a) in the management of the arts or (b) with a management consulting firm (Bazerman, 1990). A person who is interested in art and who considers music as a career is more typical (again, more representative) of the kind of person we would expect to become an arts manager. However, the number of job openings available with consulting firms is many times greater than the number of positions available in arts management, suggesting that the MBA student would be much more likely to end up working for a management consulting firm, regardless of how typical the student is of what we believe an arts manager should be like. If you were asked whether an MBA student would be more likely to take a job in the arts or with a consulting firm, you would probably (and correctly) assume the latter. However, if information that appears to be typical for a category (the student's description in the above example) alters your decision, then representativeness has biased your judgment.

Suppose a company computer skills training course is available, and you need to decide whether people in your department would benefit from attending. While pondering the possibility, you encounter one of your staff, find out that he has little computer expertise, and decide that all employees should participate in the training program. If your sample of one was typical of the computer skill level for your department, then your decision was most likely a good one. However, if you incorrectly assumed that the one employee (or even a relatively small number of the entire staff) represents the skill level of your entire department (and, in fact, most of your workers don't require further training because they are extremely computer literate), then your generalization of the real situation was mistaken. We often misperceive the randomness of events and conclude a pattern exists when what we've experienced is simply chance. The human mind is geared toward making sense of the world by bringing order out of chaos (which is why we see figures when we view stellar constellations or animal shapes when we observe clouds floating overhead).

People (especially gamblers) frequently fall prey to this type of bias. We lost six poker hands in a row, so the odds are that we'll win the next one. The last five part-time employees we hired turned out to be incompetent and ineffective, so the next one surely cannot be another lemon. A fair coin has landed on tails four times in a row, so the next coin toss is much more likely to result in heads. Representativeness leads decision makers to believe that events in a series should balance out, even though what has happened in the past has no impact on what occurs in the future (Tversky & Kahneman, 1971). Chance is not self-correcting; a run of successes (or failures) does not imply an equivalent probability of things going the other way.

Representativeness biases our decision processes to assume that things will even out, and it can also influence our thinking in the opposite direction (Gilovich, 1993). A friend tells you that one out of every five people in the world is Chinese, but of the several hundreds of people you know, not one is Chinese; therefore, your friend must be incorrect. In a like manner, many of us believe that success leads to further success, whereas failure breeds additional failure. Although this may indeed be true under certain circumstances (such as successful investments allowing additional investments and notoriety resulting in increased publicity), in many situations (such as gambling and other unrelated sequential events), it is not. Most people (especially sports enthusiasts) believe in the phenomenon of the "hot hand," the idea that people who are experiencing a successful streak (who are "in the groove") are more likely to continue to be successful than someone who is not having an extended run of success (who has gone cold). For example, if your favorite sports player has just made his last five shots, would you believe he was more or less likely to make the next one? Ask anyone who is interested in sports (either as a player or an observer), and the invariable answer is that the hot hand exists: Players who are experiencing a successful streak are more likely to continue in their success than players who are not on a roll. However, the hot hand is a myth

(Gilovich, Vallone, & Tversky, 1985). Research has convincingly demonstrated that immediately prior event success (for example, if the shot scored) has no bearing on the likelihood of the upcoming event (the next shot). Sports enthusiasts deny this finding because all of us can recollect seeing streaks where a player has experienced four, five, and even more successes in a row—we have witnessed the hot hand with our own eyes. However, representativeness has biased our perception. Think of flipping a fair coin 20 times. We all know that, on average, we should get an equal number of heads and tails. We would never expect, however, that a tails will immediately follow every heads toss. In fact, out of 20 tosses, a 50-50 chance exists that at least four tosses in a row will be heads (or tails), a 25% probability exists that five tosses in a row will be the same, and a 10% chance exists that we will get a streak of six in a row. If an average player shoots about 50% (makes his shot half the time) and takes 20 shots during a game, then a reasonable chance exists that a streak of 4, 5, or even 6 shots (or, unfortunately, an equal number of misses) in a row should happen quite frequently. We see five successes one after another, and our minds categorize the event as an example of a hot hand, rather than as a simple streak expectable from chance probability. Our orderly human brain seeks to organize and categorize what we see, to determine cause when we see effect. Our ever vigilant attention senses a pattern when a sequence of events happens (or fails to happen in the average gambler's case), and the categorization system used by the brain classifies the random series of events as a streak. A random presentation forms itself into something we can interpret (like seeing a face when we look at the moon).

Another example of representativeness is demonstrated by the sentence below. As you read the following text, count the number of *f*s you come across.

> Finished files are the result of years of scientific study combined with the experience of many years.

Did you find three *f*s? How about four? Maybe five? Are there six *f*s in the sentence (or possibly even more)? Try counting the *f*s again. The correct answer is six. Many people fail to include the letter *f* in the word *of*, which is used three times in the sentence. The reason we miss the *f* in *of*, even after repeated attempts, is that the mind categorizes *f* as an "eff" sound (like the *f* in Frank). However, the *f* in *of* sounds like a *v* (for example, the *v* in love), and our eyes skip over each *of* because it is not typical of what we expect an *f* to be. If you miscounted the letter *f* in the example above, then representativeness biased your perception.

Another type of categorization effect is *regression to the mean* (Kahneman & Tversky, 1973). Your company had record earnings last year. How likely is it that it can repeat again this year? Or conversely, your company suffered its worst losses ever. How likely is it that the upcoming year will be as bad? A salesperson has a banner year, selling three times as much as any previous year. Would you expect that level of performance to continue in the future? Your company implemented strict policy measures following an unusually high amount of employee theft, and stealing decreased over the next several months. Was the new policy successful? The above are examples of how extreme events can influence our judgment. Any repeated, observable phenomenon, such as company performance, individual sales, and employee theft, has an average or base rate of occurrence that would be typical for the event. For example, your company profits generally average an 8% growth rate per year, but last year, profits grew by 125% (or last year, the company suffered an extreme loss of 25%). A salesperson averages 10 major sales a year, but last year had a whopping total of 30 (or suffered a bad year with only 2 sales). Your company averages 2% of net sales in employee theft every year, but last year, thefts were an exceptional 11% (or last year, there were an unbelievably low number of employee thefts). Many factors (company policies, economic conditions, weather, competition, governmental regulations, new technology, and so on) can combine to influence a given outcome (such as company profits, personal sales, or employee theft). Some of these factors may have a positive impact whereas others might be negative, and over time, the effects tend to balance out. However, several chance factors may connect, resulting in an unlikely but still possible outcome. When we witness an exceptional chance occurrence of this kind, we generally fail to take into account its extreme nature when predicting subsequent events (Kahneman & Tversky, 1973).

To understand how regression to the mean works, imagine playing your favorite sport or activity. You typically have an average level of performance (which may be fairly high or low compared to others), but every once in a while, everything just seems to go right and you play exceptionally well (or possibly everything goes wrong and you feel as though you can do nothing right). On a day when all the little pieces fit together well, you can probably outperform a superior player. Of course, on a day when you can't quite get into the rhythm, a lesser player can beat you. Or imagine taking a test. While you might be fairly knowledgeable about the material and fairly good at taking tests, it is unlikely that you would expect to get a perfect score. However, it may be that all the factors that combine to influence your test-taking ability on a given day (such as how much sleep you got, the amount of anxiety you feel, your intuitive hunches, and so forth) are in your favor, and you do not miss a single question. Unlikely but possible. Or things might go the other way. You got a speeding ticket on the way to the test and are feeling very emotional, the person behind you has an irritating cough that distracts you at inconvenient times, you couldn't sleep because a neighbor was blaring his stereo, and a host of other negative factors all combine to interfere with your test-taking ability, resulting in a lower score than you normally would achieve. In either case (the perfect score or the poor performance), the next time you take a similar test, you can expect the outcome to match your actual skill level more closely. In other words, many of the factors that happened to mix in your favor (or against you) will not be present next time, and the result will be more indicative of your actual ability. The same is true for other types of events. Although doing well, a student who graduated valedictorian from high school does not perform at the same high level in college. A record-setting team fails to repeat the following season. A student who scored a perfect 1600 on his SAT proves to be a major disappointment after being admitted into graduate school. A business with phenomenal growth its first year is unable to maintain the same rate of growth the next few years. An athlete who breaks the record her rookie year doesn't even get close to the same level of performance throughout her career. Although we can generally predict future events with some degree of accuracy using historical trends, we often allow an unusual outcome (like a record-breaking year or an unbelievably bad season) to bias our prediction of subsequent events.

One of your salespeople has an exceptional year, and you reward him with bonuses, a promotion, praise, and recognition. The following year, he doesn't do as well (his sales are more typical of his previous sales efforts). Does this imply your reward attempts were ineffective? Or the salesperson had a dismal year compared to his usual efforts, so you chew him out, make him work more hours, and threaten him with dismissal if things don't improve. Lo and behold, the next year his sales improve (are similar to previous seasons). Does this mean threats and fear tactics are effective? Although your management style may have had some influence, a more likely explanation is a return to a more realistic (or typical) level of performance. We are sometimes aware of regression to the mean effects. When we see an athlete break a record (for example, the number of home runs batted in a season, number of points shot in a game, or number of completed passes in a row), we intuitively anticipate that the same level of performance is unlikely to continue the next time we watch the player perform. We recognize that the event was so unlikely (although possible because we observed it ourselves) that a more realistic performance will result next time. The *Sports Illustrated* jinx is a prime example of the regression to the mean effect (Gilovich, 1993). A common sports myth predicts that athletes depicted on the cover of *Sports Illustrated* will be cursed once they become a cover story; whatever success they experienced will evaporate, and bad luck will follow. Of course, what these sports figures fear is true: They are unlikely to have as good a year after appearing on the cover. However, rather than a curse, this is simply statistical regression. Notoriety and newsworthiness result from extraordinary performance, and more normal levels of performance almost always follow exceptional displays of skill.

A further example of regression to the mean effects is demonstrated by the national best-seller *In Search of Excellence* (Peters & Waterman, 1982). At the time, America's best-run companies included Bechtel, Boeing, Caterpillar Tractor, Dana, Delta Airlines, Digitial Equipment, Emerson Electric, Fluor, Hewlett-Packard, IBM, Johnson & Johnson, McDonald's, Proctor & Gamble, and 3M. However, many of the factors that combined to allow these companies to be examples of excellence have regressed to the average, and the companies' achievements since the early 1980s reflect a more typical level of performance. By its very nature, excellence is extraordinary and unlikely to occur at a comparable level in the future. In a similar fashion, a "great general" might be one who won five consecutive battles, but out of hundreds of generals fighting several battles, it would not be surprising to find some (although admittedly few) who have a sequence of victories purely by chance (of course, the longer the streak, the less likely it is to occur by chance). Categorization effects such as regression to the mean have been implicated in the high rate of business failures, unfavorable personnel hiring decisions, and nonconservative risk decisions in disciplines such as certified public accounting (Gilovich, 1993).

Categorization effects bias our decision making because we assume past outcomes are typical of what the future will hold, and we fail to take into account the uncommon nature of extreme events when we anticipate what will happen next.

In a similar fashion, although highly unusual and coincidental events are by their very nature uncommon, they can and do occur. However, the occurrence of unlikely events does not indicate supernatural influence or the luck (or lack thereof) someone has. For example, the New York Racing Association published an "amazing" photograph of seven horses in a race finishing in their numbered order: Horse No. 1 finished first, horse No. 2 finished second, and so on to horse No. 7, which finished last. Although a sequential finish is unlikely, the odds of such an event occurring are not extreme. For a race with seven horses, the likelihood that horse No. 1 will finish first would be one in seven. Because one horse has already finished the race, the likelihood that horse No. 2 will finish second would be one in six. For all seven horses to finish in order, the probability would be:

$$1/7 \times 1/6 \times 1/5 \times 1/4 \times 1/3 \times 1/2 \times 1/1 = 1/5{,}040$$

So we would expect that on average, seven horses will finish a race in sequential order about once in every 5,000 races. Given the number of horse races occurring every day throughout all the various racetracks around the world, we should not be overly surprised that this kind of "amazing" outcome occurs relatively often.

Similarly, Hy Ruchlis (1991) relates an "unbelievable" coincidence that occurred to him. Ruchlis telephoned his friend Sam's number, and when the phone was answered, Ruchlis asked for Sam. When the person on the other end put Sam on the line, Sam said, "How did you know I was here?" Ruchlis asked, "Why? Aren't you home?" Sam responded, "No. I'm at a friend's house in my neighborhood, and no one knew I was coming here." So Ruchlis, who had intended to call his friend at home, dialed the wrong number and connected with the person he wanted to reach. Whenever Ruchlis tells this story, many people believe that the event is so unlikely that it must be an indication of supernatural intervention. Although this occurrence is extremely improbable, just how likely is it to happen? For most seven-digit telephone numbers, the first three numbers serve to connect the caller to a specific area, generally a neighborhood, county, or city. So assuming Ruchlis misdialed any of the last four digits of the telephone number, he would contact someone in the same area as his friend Sam (one of 10,000 possibilities). Furthermore, let us assume that the caller misdials on the average of once in every 50 calls (1/50), that Sam has about 10 good friends he might visit in his neighborhood (so 10 people out of 10,000 in the neighborhood is the same as 10/10,000 or 1/1,000), and that the odds that Sam will happen to be at any given friend's house at a particular time would be around 1 in 1,000 (1/1,000). For Ruchlis to reach his friend Sam as outlined above, all of these independent events have to occur together. So the probability that Sam would be at his friend's house when Ruchlis misdials could be something like:

$$1/50 \times 1/1,000 \times 1/1,000 = 1/50,000,000$$

We might reasonably expect that at least once in every 50 million phone calls, this kind of highly unusual event would occur. With hundreds of millions of phone calls being made throughout the world every day, it is very likely that a staggering coincidence like the one described above should occur to someone at some time (who just happened to be Ruchlis in this case). Unusual and seemingly unbelievable events (like someone winning the lottery twice) are bound to happen. In fact, probability states that coincidental events should happen to all of us from time to time.

The mind categorizes things to aid our retrieval. Our short-term memory and attention span focus on locating items in long-term memory to assist in our thought processes (Sylwester, 1995). Generally, the easier it is to remember something, the more common that type of event is likely to be (Tversky & Kahneman, 1974). However, an *availability* bias can occur when we recall an event not because it is more typical, frequent, or likely but instead because it is more vivid, easily imagined, or emotionally laden. For example, we are more likely to evaluate a subordinate's performance more harshly if that employee is in close proximity to our office because the worker's errors come more readily to mind than the errors of those located farther away (Strickland, 1958). When incidents of "sudden acceleration" or beach resort shark attacks are well publicized, Audi sales and travel to Florida decline because these events are easily remembered and assumed to be more likely than they actually are (Loewenstein, 1996). Does it seem strange to you that those times when you are awakened in the middle of the night, your digital clock often seems to have some pattern of numbers like 5:55, 1:23, or 4:56? Is this just extreme coincidence or is something else going on? The likely explanation is that patterned number sequences are more available from recall than nonpatterned readings. You probably see numbers such as 5:31, 1:54, or 4:13 just as often, but they don't come to mind as readily as more vivid sequences.

Which of the following groups had the larger sales volume in 1982?

- *Group A:* American Motors, Wang Laboratories, Lever Brothers, Kellog, Scott Paper
- *Group B:* Coastal, Signal Companies, Dresser Industries, Agway, McDermott

The correct answer is Group B, although most people select Group A. Even though Group B had double the sales of Group A, most people are unfamiliar with many of the names on the second list. However, Group A consists of fairly well-known names, companies that come readily to mind and are easily recognized. The names in the first group are common, everyday companies that we know, and the judgmental tendency is to assume they are larger and more profitable businesses as well. The availability bias can lead to critical mistakes in judgment, such as when a purchasing agent selects a familiar name from a list of potential suppliers only to find that the reason the name was well-known was because of the negative publicity the firm had received due to its history of extorting funds from client companies (Bazerman, 1990). Similarly, specific subordinate actions that are easier to recall (typically, the worker's most recent or most vivid behaviors) can unduly influence the employee's annual performance evaluation (either positively or negatively).

Would you predict that you are more likely to die from being struck by falling pieces of an airplane or from a shark attack? Although most people would say death by shark attack is more likely, being hit by airplane debris is 30 times more likely to kill you. Shark-related deaths are usually newsworthy items, something we are all likely to have seen reported in the media (and in the movies). Also, it is much easier for us to imagine a shark attack than it is to picture an object crushing someone as it falls from the sky. Shark attacks are more available in our memories and subsequently mislead our expectations. Similarly, more people die from diabetes than homicide, from stomach cancer than car accidents, and from lightning than tornadoes, although most of us believe just the opposite (Combs & Slovic, 1979). We tend to overemphasize the probability of things when an item is easy to recall from memory: Memories of events that are more available are presumed to be more frequent, likely, and common than other events. The vividness, emotionality, or specificity of some events means they are more accessible to retrieval, and ease of recall biases our judgments (Nisbett & Ross, 1980). As an example, do more English words start with the letter *r*, or are there more words with *r* as the third letter? Again, most people believe the first, whereas more than twice as many English words have *r* in the third position than begin with *r* (Kahneman & Tversky, 1973). Our very orderly human brain categorizes many functions (such as vocabulary words) in much the same way as a dictionary: alphabetically. Therefore, it is much easier for us to remember words beginning with a specific letter than to recollect words with letters in varying positions. Generally, memories that are more available are also those events that are more frequent, common, and likely to happen. However, in some situations, items that are easier to retrieve from memory lead to mistaken judgments concerning how likely an event is to occur.

Add the following numbers in your head, saying the sum out loud as you proceed down the column (say "1,000 plus 10 equals 1,010 plus 1,000 equals 2,010" and so on).

1,000

+

10

+

1,000

+

20

+

1,000

+

30

+

1,000

+

40

Did you find yourself saying 5,000 at the end of the problem, rather than 4,100? Again, the human mind can only juggle a limited number of items at a time, and we tend to use shortcuts to aid our decision processes. As we perform the calculation above, the number 5,000 comes to mind much more readily than the actual answer of 4,100. The availability of a more common or typical response makes it easier for us to assume that it is most likely the correct response. Facts that come readily to mind (memories that conveniently "pop into our heads" because they are more available) are used when we make judgments, but our decisions can be distorted if these events are not more applicable but simply easier to recall.

Categorization effects are subtle yet pervasive. The human mind attempts to make sense of the world and works very effectively to categorize and analyze our experiences, but our thinking processes are susceptible to systematic errors in perception. To deal with possible categorization effects, it helps if we examine our assumptions to see if decisional shortcuts have biased our thinking. Are our assumptions valid, or have we fallen prey to misinterpretation of the data? To the extent possible, we should find additional support for what we believe by using statistics and hard facts. And we need to be aware that our mind is constantly trying to sort all the sensory information it receives and form patterns and connections to our experiences. The mind efficiently organizes information to aid our decision making. However, things are not always what they appear, and sometimes, random events can appear to be ordered, coincidences do occur, and seemingly unbelievable situations can arise.

COMBATING JUDGMENTAL BIASES

Human decision makers are susceptible to systematically flawed thinking. The makeup of our incredibly complex minds and our socialization shape us into potent but imperfect problem solvers. We strive to make accurate judgments whenever possible, but we are trapped by psychological inconsistencies in how we deal with many problems. However, much of this inconsistency can be avoided (or at least minimized) if we become aware of our own biased thought processes. Understanding judgmental biases is the first step in improving our decision making.

One of the simplest and most effective ways of addressing many of our decisional errors is considering multiple alternatives before we act (Plous, 1993). Divergent perspectives allow us to consider multiple outcomes, and a simple rule in decision making is that when it comes to solving problems, more is almost always better. Not only does the consideration of multiple viewpoints limit the impact of our emotional, impulsive nature, but it also removes (or at least diminishes the impact of) the element of bias, which is causing us to look at a problem in a restricted, erroneous, or incorrect way. In addition, the steps in Table 4.1 are suggested as ways to decrease the likelihood that we will fall prey to systematically biased decision making.

SUMMARY AND REVIEW

Decision makers often use simplified rules to solve problems. Although these assumptions work well most of the time, they are susceptible to a host of judgmental biases. Selective perception occurs when we see what we want or expect to see by screening less relevant information or impressions. The primacy effect occurs when initial impressions and information carry more decisional weight than later impressions or information due to easier retrievability and recall from memory. The recency effect happens when recent impressions or information carries more decisional weight than earlier impressions and information due to vivid recall from memory. The halo effect occurs when we believe a single characteristic or attribute a person possesses is indicative of other desirable traits or characteristics.

Presentation effects can happen when the order or way in which information is presented influences our decisions. Similarly, framing effects cause decision makers to avoid risk when considering positively framed options (gains) and to seek risk when considering negatively framed situations (losses). Escalation of commitment takes place when we make decisions that continue to support previously unsuccessful courses of action because too much has been invested to quit.

Categorization effects involve how information is stored and accessed in our minds. Representativeness occurs when we perceive information as typical or representative of the class to which we have categorized it, regression to the mean happens when we tend to ignore the fact that ex-

TABLE 4.1 Avoiding Judgmental Biases

Judgmental Bias	Suggestions for Avoiding
Selective perception	Take multiple perspectives Be aware of our expectations beforehand Strive for objectivity Ask how an impartial outsider would view the situation Be honest in our assessments of why we feel the way we do toward a person or event
Impression effects	Take multiple perspectives Force ourselves to consider events before and after the ones that readily come to mind Play devil's advocate to uncover the justification for what we believe
Presentation effects	Take multiple perspectives Attempt to consider the problem before presentation information is provided Seek out other opinions and perspectives, especially from those not too close to the problem Be prepared with enough information to minimize presentation effects Be aware of how our presentation of the problem may bias the opinions of others Consider best, worst, and most likely scenarios
Framing effects	Take multiple perspectives Try to frame problems in terms of objectives we're trying to achieve Never automatically accept a given frame—always reframe and look for distortion Strive for neutrality Frame the problem from the opposite perspective and attempt to justify the new viewpoint Be aware of how our framing might influence the decisions of others
Escalation of commitment effects	Take multiple perspectives Consider arguments from others, especially from those who were not involved in the initial decision Be aware of why we are committing ourselves to a further course of action Anticipate a possible withdrawal beforehand and factor the costs of retreat into our thinking Explicitly share responsibility with others Set limits in advance and stick to them Select others who were uninvolved with the initial decision to make the new decision

TABLE 4.1 *(continued)*

Judgmental Bias	Suggestions for Avoiding
Categorization effects	Take multiple perspectives
	Examine assumptions to see if categorization may have biased our thought processes
	Support data retrieved from memory with hard facts
	Separate seemingly related items to uncover the source of their connectivity
	Be aware that random events occur and that we seek patterns where none may exist
	Recognize that coincidence does happen
	Understand that some events are more likely to occur than others

treme events are likely to be more average the next time they occur, and availability occurs when we are more likely to recall a memory due to its vividness or ease of retrieval from our minds and assume that the information is more typical or likely because it is easily imagined.

5 | Perceptions of Risk and Decision Making

A s outlined earlier, the way we frame a situation influences our decisions. Our responses are different when we perceive decisions in terms of losses rather than gains—we seek risk when facing guaranteed losses but avoid risk under conditions of guaranteed gain (Kahneman & Tversky, 1973). But what is risk? What makes some decisions more risky than others?

Most of us agree that risk essentially deals with uncertainty. We characterize risky decisions as those that entail greater amounts of uncertainty (such as "a shot in the dark"), whereas "safer" decisions are generally viewed as those whose outcomes are more predictable and likely (such as "a sure thing"). All of us, especially those in business, are constantly faced with making decisions that will result in uncertain outcomes (MacCrimmon & Wehrung, 1986). To manage risk, decision makers gather as much relevant information as possible to manipulate future outcomes and minimize the odds against them (Amit & Wernerfelt, 1990). We use information to determine the probability or likelihood of an event occurring. For example, history indicates a company's stock price usually increases 75% of the time if quarterly sales earnings are up at least 5%, so we decide to purchase stock after hearing the latest quarterly figures. Or the weatherman says a 50-50 chance of rain exists for tomorrow, so we decide to reschedule an event for a later date.

Although uncertainty is a basic component of risky decisions, risk is more complex than simply determining the odds of an event occurring. Our perceptions of risk are influenced by a number of other factors as well (Yates & Stone, 1992). In addition to uncertainty, perceptions of risk appear to be determined by our expectation of the potential gains and/or losses involved, how the decision is framed, and the amount of personal exposure we believe we are facing (Williams & Y. Wong, 1999) (see Table 5.1).

UNCERTAINTY

When we make an important decision, we are rarely completely certain what the result will be. Whether we're thinking about accepting a blind date or contemplating starting a new business venture, most of our decisions will be filled with uncertainty. We try to cope with uncertainty by accumulating as much pertinent information as possible, but even then, we can never be sure of the outcome beforehand. Life is complex, and important decisions tend to be multifaceted, so the entire range of possible consequences can rarely be completely assessed. However, we can still improve our problem solving by acknowledging the existence of doubt and uncertainty. And we can prepare ourselves by understanding the various consequences that might occur, their probability of occurring, and the impact they are likely to have on our lives.

As uncertainty increases, decisions become more risky (MacCrimmon & Wehrung, 1986; Sitkin & Pablo, 1992; Williams & Y. Wong, 1999; Yates & Stone, 1992). Although all risky decisions involve some uncertainty, uncertainty itself can take several forms. We may be uncertain as to which outcomes are possible, we may be unclear about how likely it is that certain outcomes will occur, or we may not be sure how outcomes can be influenced by ourselves or others (March, 1994; Yates & Stone, 1992). For example, our decision is risky because we are uncertain what might result from our actions. Or we have narrowed down the possible outcomes from our risky decision, but we just don't know which one is more (or less) likely to occur. Or we know what might happen, but we are not sure what we (or others) might do to increase the likelihood that a desired outcome will result or that an undesirable consequence can be avoided. As uncer-

TABLE 5.1 Elements of Risk

Element	*Example*
Uncertainty	It's a long shot. I'd say it's a 50-50 chance. We predict a 30% probability.
Gains	I could win a fortune. We won't get much out of this deal. We could be sitting pretty.
Losses	It's no big deal if I lose. This could wipe us out. We can survive if it's not too bad.
Framing	Our company is rolling smoothly, so why take a chance? This ship is going to sink fast if we don't turn things around.
Personal exposure	If this works out, my future with the company is secure. This will really put a dent in my career if things go bad.

tainty about potential outcomes, probabilities, and controllability increase, our perceptions of risk increase as well.

To cope with uncertainty, we strive to gather appropriate information. Knowledge about what has occurred in the past or what is happening at present can assist in making projections and predictions about what might happen in the future. Much of the information we use to make risky decisions comes from our experience-based intuition, that emotional reaction suggesting the correct course of action (Simon, 1987). Our history of making similar risky decisions (both successfully and unsuccessfully) carries a great deal of weight in swaying our risk judgments. Generally, decision makers who have had exposure to comparable risk-related experiences in the past are better able to gather and use relevant information in making similar risky decisions (Kirschenbaum, 1992). Expertise in a given area increases the likelihood of recognizing and interpreting meaningful information, which is why we often seek professional advice (from doctors, lawyers, and so on) when confronted with risky decisions.

We dislike uncertainty and try to avoid it or minimize it whenever possible. Although some decision makers try to cope by ignoring uncertainty (Dawes, 1988), most of us deal with uncertainty by attempting to control it (Williams & Luthans, 1992). In fact, we are so concerned with controlling uncertainty that we believe that we can actually influence chance events (Langer, 1975). For example, those who gamble in the lottery believe they have more control over winning because they choose their own numbers (Bazerman, 1990), and employees believe they can control uncertainty if they are allowed to choose their own rewards (Williams & Luthans, 1992). Uncertainty and unpredictability make us uncomfortable. We gather meaningful information to lessen the uncertainty we feel, but even in situations where our risky decisions are completely determined by chance, we still feel a need to control uncertainty by any means possible (Brigham, 1979; Williams, 1990).

POTENTIAL GAINS AND LOSSES

Another factor influencing our perceptions of risk is how significant the potential outcomes might be. The greater the likely loss, the higher the implied risk. In addition, higher potential losses must be counterbalanced with a relatively greater possibility of gain (MacCrimmon & Wehrung, 1986; Sitkin & Pablo, 1992; Yates & Stone, 1992). When assessing risk, we would obviously prefer larger anticipated gains to smaller gains and smaller potential losses to larger losses. Riskiness increases as possible returns become smaller and potential losses appear larger relative to one another. Purchasing a lottery ticket is not perceived to be risky by most of us because the potential loss (usually about a dollar) is minor when weighed against the potential gain (sometimes several million dollars). Similarly, a decision to advertise a new product on the company's Web page is probably not perceived as too risky because the anticipated gains (increased sales revenue, brand recognition, and other positives) are much higher than potential losses (the expense of designing and uploading the appropriate content).

A demonstration of how potential gains and losses influence our perceptions of risk comes from our attitude toward illegal activities. For example, assume that performing an unlawful activity such as illegally dumping our untreated sewage into the neighborhood river has the potential of reaping tremendous monetary benefits for the company due to the extremely high amount we must spend to assure our waste is environmentally safe. Although this is a criminal act, what is the likelihood that we will go to jail? First, our illegal activity must be uncovered. Then, we must be apprehended for committing the crime, convicted of the activity in a court of law, sentenced to serve time in prison, and finally incarcerated. Although the probability of us actually going to jail may be extremely slim and the potential gains (both personal and organizational) might be potentially very large, we probably (although not definitely) would still be unlikely to commit the crime. The improbable outcome (the potential loss) of being incarcerated is perceived to be so distasteful (even though it is extremely unlikely) that we willingly forgo anticipated gains in favor of a solution that entails a less extreme negative outcome. Similarly, we believe it is reasonable to expend great effort to achieve some goals, even though the probability of actually attaining them is small, if the potential gains are viewed as very attractive and the potential losses are believed to be minimal (or at least acceptable).

All decision makers prefer positive outcomes to negative ones. Unfortunately, we are geared toward believing that desirable consequences are more likely to occur to us than negative events (Lerner, 1970). Whether we are predicting how likely it is that what we want to happen will actually occur, estimating which of several desirable outcomes will most likely result, or wagering on an advantageous outcome, we tend to believe that good things are more likely than bad (Plous, 1993). Positive outcomes are believed to be more likely, so we overestimate the probability that desirable things will happen to us when considering risky alternatives. And when we believe higher potential gains are possible and outcomes will be more positive, we are much more likely to choose riskier courses of action (Williams & Y. Wong, 1999). Many of us, when faced with risky decisions, intuitively seek out uninvolved (but knowledgeable) outsiders for consultation to counter our tendency to maximize the positive and minimize the negative.

The more extreme the potential outcome, the riskier a decision is believed to be. An "all-or-nothing" gamble would be an example of an extremely risky decision because gains and losses are both maximized. Some decisions we encounter are of this caliber. We elect to take the company in a new strategic direction, changing how and with whom we do business. We accept the high-risk, high-opportunity job offer at the expense of our safe and certain current employment. We invest extensive funds in a project that has the possibility of reaping huge benefits (or alternatively losing our entire investment). Any risky option that may result in significant losses fails to be considered seriously unless it is counterbalanced by a substantial and highly desirable reward (Sitkin & Pablo, 1992). However, risk does not just include negative outcomes such as losses. Choosing between possible positive outcomes can also be perceived as risky (March & Shapira, 1987). If we face a decision where all the options are gains, we would still view the situation as risky if one (or more) of the outcomes is significantly more attractive than the others. Even if all of the applicants for the vacant position in your department look promising, you may perceive your choice as risky if one or more have the potential of being star performers, but you can't be sure which one(s). When you know that you could win the sports car if you select the right door (and some lesser prize otherwise), then you perceive your choice as a risky one. Similarly, selecting from among possible negative outcomes can be perceived as very risky if one (or more) alternative has the potential of minimizing our loss by producing the least amount of damage. All the treatments available for cancer entail risk, but perceptions of risk increase when patients must consider a "promising" but untested therapy as opposed to more traditional treatments.

INFORMATION FRAMING

Imagine that your company is in the midst of a complicated legal battle. Your lawyers advise you that if the case ends up in court, a 50-50 chance exists that it could cost the company as much as $1 million. You have just received an offer from the opposing party expressing a willingness to settle out of court for $500,000. Would you accept the offer?

As mentioned previously, the way risk is framed is another factor influencing how we decide (Williams & Y. Wong, 1999). If the situation is identified as one where the company is faced with a sure loss of $500,000 (the settlement figure), then decision makers are more likely to seek a risky course of action by going to court in hopes of minimizing losses. Losing $500,000 is bad, and losing $1 million is even worse, but we'll risk the possibility of losing more on the chance that we may not lose anything; we're willing to risk greater losses if we might avoid any loss at all. On the other hand, if the situation is identified as one where the company is faced with a definite gain of $500,000 (the amount saved of the $1 million that could be lost in court), then decision makers are more likely to avoid risk by accepting the sure thing rather than risking a legal battle. A gain of $500,000 is good, and even though it will cost us $500,000 to achieve this positive outcome, we are unwilling to risk this definite gain on the chance that we might obtain even more in the courtroom (by not losing anything). How we perceive the acts, outcomes, and contingencies associated with a particular choice exerts control over our decision processes (Tversky & Kahneman, 1981).

To see why the formulation of a decision influences the way we respond, we need to understand how we view the usefulness or value of what we might gain or lose. If you were offered a choice between a sure thing of $100 and the flip of a fair coin for the chance to win $200 (or to win nothing), which would you select? Most people prefer the sure gain rather than taking the risk for twice as much. Although $200 is more desirable than $100, $100 is more useful (has more value) to you than a 50-50 chance of $200. Would you risk a guaranteed $100 for a 50-50 chance at $300? How about $400? Or $1,000? As the amount increases, more and more people are willing to chance the coin toss because the amount to be gained has more usefulness (again, is more valuable) than the sure thing.

However, the situation reverses when we consider losses rather than gains. If you were offered the choice between a guaranteed loss of $100 and the flip of a fair coin for the chance to lose $200 or to lose nothing at all, which would you choose? Most people prefer to take the risk. Although we don't want to lose $200, we've pictured the situation as one where we have already lost $100 *but we might not lose anything at all.* Although a loss of $200 hurts more than a loss of $100, losing nothing is even more appealing (again, it has more value) to us than a sure loss of $100. Would you risk a sure loss of $100 for a 50-50 chance to lose either $300 or nothing? How about $400? Or $1,000? Again, as the amount increases, fewer decision makers are willing to chance the coin toss because the amount has less usefulness than the guaranteed loss. Risky decision *framing* is controlled by how the problem is viewed, filtered by the norms, habits, and characteristics of the decision maker (Tversky & Kahneman, 1981).

As another example of how framing influences our risk perceptions, imagine that you loaned a colleague at work $100 with the assurance that you would be repaid within a month. Unfortunately, your coworker received a transfer to another state, and you lost all contact with him. You've forgotten all about the loan, but 2 years later, you happen to run into the same individual at a regional meeting. To your surprise, he pulls out his wallet and offers to repay the loan on the spot. As he extends the money to your outstretched hand, he says, "Wait a minute. I'll give you a choice. You can either accept the $100 (the sure gain) or I'll let you flip a coin and if it's heads I'll give you $200, but if it's tails I keep the money." Which do you choose? Most decision makers avoid the gamble and take the sure thing.

Now, turn the situation around. Imagine that your coworker loaned *you* $100 and then he was transferred out of state before you could repay him. Two years pass, and you run into him at the regional meeting. He reminds you of the $100 you owe him (and you feel ashamed for having forgotten), but as you are about to write a check to reimburse him for the loan, he says, "Wait a minute. I'll give you a choice. You can either give me the $100 (the sure loss), or I'll let you flip a coin and if it's heads you give me $200, but if it's tails you keep the money." Which do you choose? Most decision makers accept the gamble and try to avoid the sure loss.

When faced with risky decisions, we place more value on the possibility of avoiding loss (by incurring potentially greater costs) over the acceptance of an assured loss. Decision makers dislike losses and will take risks to minimize and, they hope, avoid them. The pain and discomfort associated with losing a given amount is more extreme than the pleasure experienced by gaining the same amount. For example, in bargaining and negotiation situations, parties often view their own concessions as much more important and critical than the concessions they have gained from the other side (Quattrone & Tversky, 1988). When things are going well, decision makers believe that fewer risks should be taken, and they expect riskier choices to be made if a company is failing (March & Shapira, 1987). In positive situations, where performance is above some desired target level, potential gains are seen as less attractive whereas potential losses loom large because they may drop performance below the established standard, which leads to risk avoidance. However, in negative situations, where performance is below some preferred level, anticipated gains appear more attractive, and risk seeking increases in an attempt to attain desired standards. As an example, a general who is losing a war is much more likely to decide on a risky military venture, especially one that may reverse the situation, than a general who is on the winning side.

PERSONAL INVOLVEMENT

Another factor influencing risk perceptions is whether risks are perceived as personally relevant. Businesspeople make risky decisions all the time, but not all of the outcomes of the decisions they make affect them personally. Some risky decisions may carry personal accountability if we are recognized as being responsible for the decision. The extent to which decision makers are personally affected by events arising from their risky decisions is important because risk aversion appears to increase as risk-related outcomes become more personal in nature (Williams & Y. Wong, 1999). For example, managers are more inclined to take risks when making business rather than personal decisions (March & Shapira, 1987). Similarly, employees are less likely to seek risk when personal consequences are high (MacCrimmon & Wehrung, 1986). As risky decisions become more important to the decision maker personally, risk-seeking behavior tends to decrease.

The amount of responsibility we feel for a given risky decision influences our actions (Whyte, 1991). When evaluating risky options, we consider how much impact the likely outcome will have on us personally (our career, our job, our work situation, and so on). Risky courses are more likely to be selected when we are making decisions for others (for the company) than when we are making similar decisions that affect us personally and directly. So managers who tend to be risk-averse at home routinely select risky options in their business lives (March & Shapira, 1987). When personal consequences are high, decision makers tend to be more conservative in their appraisals and in their actions than when personal consequences are not as important (MacCrimmon & Wehrung, 1986). However, if the result of our decision turns out to be negative and we feel personally responsible, we are also more likely to continue to pursue a failing course of action in hopes that things will improve (Staw, 1976).

A staff meeting is called to discuss various risky projects that have high potential payoffs. After evaluating the alternatives, one option looks especially promising to you. Although the project appears to be risky, you believe the likely gains are worth the risk. Would your willingness to support the risky project be influenced by the amount of personal involvement you anticipated? Would you consider the situation differently if your boss asked you to accept personal responsibility for the risky assignment by becoming the project manager? What if you were just asked your opinion, and the actual project would be handled by someone else? Generally, we tend to be more conservative in our decision making when we believe we will be personally involved in the outcome than when we believe otherwise: The more accountable we feel, the more thorough are our analytical processes (Tetlock, Sitka, & Boettger, 1989). Important and meaningful decisions that affect us personally carry a great deal of weight and are held to a higher standard of acceptability. However, even though decision makers tend to make safer decisions when held personally accountable for the result, additional factors such as our beliefs in how much control we exercise and how competent we feel in our abilities also moderate the degree to which we will choose a riskier course of action (Williams & Y. Wong, 1999).

SUMMARY AND REVIEW

Risk is a multidimensional perception (see Figure 5.1). Generally, when people talk about risk, they mean the amount of uncertainty or lack of predictability concerning the outcome of a decision. Decisions are also seen as risky depending on the amount of gains and/or losses possible—how much can we gain compared to what might be lost? Also, risk involves framing because we tend to be more risk seeking when we view our situation as negative relative to some predetermined standard of evaluation and more risk avoiding when we see things as more positive relative to that standard. Finally, decisions that are more personally relevant to us are believed to be riskier because we are personally involved.

Our perceptions of risk are determined by the amount of uncertainty present, our expectations of gains and/or losses, how we frame the decision, and the amount of personal involvement we feel (Williams & Y. Wong, 1999). These factors combine to form an assessment of how risky or safe we believe the situation to be. In addition, our interpretation of these dimensions is likely to influence the extent to which we believe we can actively control risk (Strickland, Lewicki, & Katz, 1966). Uncertainty, potential gains and losses, framing, and personal involvement not only determine how risky we believe a decision is, but also influence the extent to which we believe we can exert control (Langer, 1975). For example, we generally believe risk is manageable and subject to influence

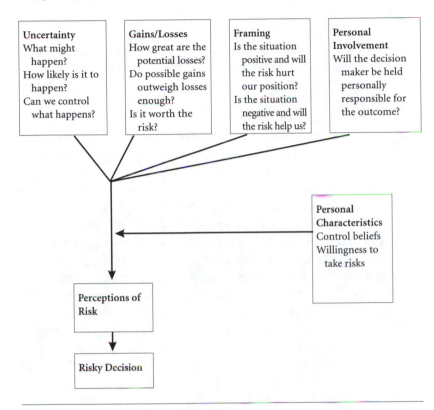

Figure 5.1. Risk and Decision Making

(MacCrimmon & Wehrung, 1986), and we actively seek to adjust and control risk decisions to make them more attractive (March & Shapira, 1987). Whenever possible, we attempt to modify risk by attacking the problem from multiple directions to improve the odds. Although we may recognize that a particular course of action is riskier than an alternative, we may still decide to pursue the risky option if we also believe we will be able to exert an element of control over possible outcomes. Uncertainty may be high, possible gains and losses may be maximized, we may frame the decision in a way that encourages risk, and we may feel intense personal involvement; and we may still decide on a riskier course of action if we also believe that we can control some or all of the factors involved. If we anticipate that uncertainty can be lessened by gaining appropriate information, that losses can be avoided and gains can be maximized by actively controlling all aspects of the situation, that the decisional frame is correct and justified, and that we will be able to minimize any negative personal impact resulting from the decision, we may willingly pursue risky options.

Although risk can never be eliminated from our decision making, we can attempt to minimize its impact. Uncertainty will likely be present, but we generally only need to focus on those aspects that might significantly influence the consequences of our decisions. Furthermore, assigning realistic chances to key uncertain events allows us to weigh and compare consequences. Understanding how we perceive potential gains and losses, whether they will be major or minor, and the tradeoffs associated with each can also decrease our feelings of risk. Is the gain worth the potential loss? Is the potential loss worth the gain? We also need to know how we are framing the risky problem. Is our perception of the problem tainting our risk preferences such that we are either more or less willing to take risky chances? If we attempt to view our problems from multiple vantage points and strive to see decisions from both positive and negative perspectives, we decrease the likelihood that framing will bias our thinking processes. If we have clarified the likely outcomes and determined that our decision will (or will not) have an important impact on us personally, do we allow this expectation to influence our actions? What if the opposite were true and we were not (or were) likely to be held responsible for the consequences of our decisions? Would we behave differently? If so, do we understand why, and can we justify the reasoning behind our position?

Part II

Understanding and
Improving Critical
Thinking Skills

6 | Thinking Critically

How We Know What We Know

S uppose you are responsible for purchasing something for your company (let's say office computers) and are assigned the task of deciding which of the many options available the company should buy. You are somewhat familiar with computers (maybe enough to get yourself into trouble), but you feel you need more information to make a reasoned decision. You visit a mass retailer of electronic goods and ask the salesperson which choice she would recommend to meet the department's requirements. Armed with this knowledge, you visit another computer store and request a recommendation, which differs from the first suggestion. You travel to a third outlet and are given still another proposal. Feeling somewhat confused, you gather sales information from various sources (brochures, media advertisements, Web pages, and so on) to assist your decision making but find that each manufacturer argues its product is the one that will best meet your needs. Although you would like to believe all the facts and figures presented to you, you also realize that every offering cannot be superior and therefore scrutinize the information available with some degree of skepticism. After all, you understand that product manufacturers might have a motive to shade the truth and to present their brand in the most favorable light: They benefit from selling to you regardless of whether you benefit to the same degree. It would be easiest to believe what others tell you and make a quick choice because being skeptical requires additional effort. However, you also realize that if you don't exercise at least a minimum amount of skepticism, your gullibility may lead to problems later. So how do you decide what to do?

Critical thinking requires skepticism. For our purposes, critical thinking means being able to build and understand a reasoned argument, to apply skepticism to what we hear, and especially to recognize an incorrect or fraudulent assertion. Critical thinking involves confirming the "facts" as we understand them, eliciting knowledgeable debate regarding the evidence, verifying the source of authority for what we hear, generating alternative explanations, and testing what we believe. Thinking critically requires hard work and time we could be spending doing other important activities. Is skepticism worth the effort? Although a little gullibility might lead to some inaccurate decisions, surely its effects can't be that serious, can they?

For decades, people (especially doctors) have stated that smoking results in cancer. Tobacco companies readily admit that cigarettes and cancer are related, but they have repeatedly argued that relationship does not mean causality. They reason that something else, possibly hereditary, leads some people to develop cancer, and these same individuals tend to take up smoking. Therefore, many people who have a drive to smoke also have a genetic likelihood of contracting cancer. The cigarette industry maintains that smoking does not cause cancer. Tobacco companies have historically insisted that their objective is to address these fanatical assumptions, fallacious rumors, unsupported claims, and unscientific statements and set aside in the minds of millions the false conviction that cigarette smoking causes cancer and other diseases.

Tobacco companies (as well as many individual smokers) agree that smoking and cancer are correlated, but they disagree that smoking causes disease. They argue that science just hasn't located the underlying factor that causes both smoking addiction and cancer. Because the tobacco industry grosses billions of dollars every year, they would certainly appear to have the resources to confirm or deny whether their product was a hazard, wouldn't they? And wouldn't the safety of one's product be the overriding concern for a corporation, because companies surely would not prefer profits to physical injury and death, would they? Besides, doesn't the government regulate hazardous materials and look out for consumer well-being? All of these arguments appear to be sound, suggesting that tobacco may not cause cancer as cigarette makers assert. However, because the consequences are potentially great (some would say life-and-death), a prospective smoker would want to critically analyze the information available and reach a sound decision. So how would we determine whether cigarette smoke actually causes cancer? To whom do we give credence and why?

What if you were informed that when nearly identical mice are randomly selected and either have their backs painted with cigarette tar or not, the mice receiving the cigarette tar have several times the amount of cancer as the non-tar mice, a rate so much higher that it is astronomically unlikely to have been caused by chance? Or what if you were told that incidents of cancer (as well as emphysema, bronchitis, and other cardiovascular diseases) increase proportionately with the amount of cigarette smoke inhaled, whereas among those who don't inhale cigarette smoke, cancer levels remain about the same as for the population at large? One question you might ask is, How reliable are the findings? In fact, this is exactly the approach taken by the tobacco industry in the early 1950s. Six major corporations began a public relations campaign disparaging research findings when it was reported that cigarette tar resulted in cancerous malignancies. Many (smokers and nonsmokers alike) believed the corporate assertions.

Smoking certainly doesn't benefit the cigarette user, regardless of what the tobacco industry would like us to believe. Before they decide to take up smoking (or if they are contemplating quitting), critical thinkers would gather as much relevant information as possible, consider the sources for that information and the underlying motivations behind what is reported, determine the truthfulness of any claims as much as possible, consider alternative explanations and their degree of fit with the existing data, and test the conviction of their decision as much as necessary. Quite a lot of work just to make a decision, but failure to think critically could have important consequences for us. Again, how substantial are the consequences and how important is the need for us to think critically about our decisions? Is a little gullibility really that bad?

Many people, especially those in Far Eastern countries, believe that powder made from the ground-up horn of the black rhinoceros can relieve headaches, cure certain illnesses, and increase sexual virility. Even if these claims are unfounded, surely it can't hurt to believe them, can it? Does this belief cause any harm? Estimates suggest that 90% of the rhinoceros population was decimated by poachers during a 15-year period, and only a few thousand rhinos are left in the world (Martin, 1981). Examples abound of black marketing in other products made from endangered species. What about our spiritual beliefs? Religious beliefs are a personal matter, and surely a little superstition and gullibility are permissible. However, when mildly ill children perish due to starvation and malnutrition because their parents' philosophy calls for fasting and forbids medical treatment, the cost of a lack of skepticism becomes all too clear (Gilovich, 1993). Offering heartfelt prayers over children with cholera will not save their lives, whereas administering 500 milligrams of antibiotic medicine (such as tetracycline) every 12 hours will. False beliefs can have disastrous results and even kill us. We act on the basis of information presented to us, and our actions can have important (even deadly) consequences. For many decisions, it pays to be skeptical and think critically.

Much of the information bombarding us is designed to influence the way we think and act. Advertisers, for example, are rarely concerned primarily with truth. Advertising (as well as other types of persuasive arguments) is designed to arouse, sustain, and direct consumer behavior, to get us to purchase a specific product or service. Sometimes (possibly most of the time), the interests of the advertisers (generating sales) are not met by providing potential customers with enough useful information to make an informed decision. Critical thinking requires that we educate ourselves about all the facts, not just those being supplied to us by people attempting to persuade us toward a particular course of action.

As critical thinkers, we are not passive acquirers of information. We have solid reasons and justifications for accepting or rejecting claims put to us. As critical thinkers, we are aware of our own attitudes and beliefs, and we realize that these elements filter the way we see and respond to the world. Are our values and attitudes biasing our beliefs and influencing our objectivity? Does our opinion carry emotional overtones? If we actively apply critical thinking skills, we must be willing to acknowledge that some of our preciously held beliefs are possibly in error, and we must be ready to alter our stand if convincing evidence is presented, regardless of how personally appealing our opinions may be. We proceed with intellectual caution, but we must be open to new points of view. However, the burden of proof lies with the presenter of new claims, and we require convincing evidence. As we consider evidence, we keep in mind the credibility of the source: Is this source reliable? What reasons do we have to accept this source? Is the presenter biased, and will others benefit if our opinion is swayed? As we consider the evidence, we keep in mind that alternative explanations are possible and even likely. Does a different explanation make more sense than the argument being presented? How sound is the evidence, and how might we gather information on our own that disconfirms what is being presented? Critical thinkers actively engage in testing the facts by poking holes in all arguments, even our own. Awareness of our own socially acquired limitations and internal standards, careful consideration of the trustworthiness of the source of new information, scrutiny of potential and likely alternative explanations of the evidence presented to us, and consideration of the correctness of evidence and the testing of claims are tools required for us to think critically and act appropriately.

ATTITUDES AND BELIEFS

The essence of believing something is believing that it is true. Obviously, if we were convinced that something we believed was false, we would no longer believe it. However, if we honestly consider our past experiences, we can all come up with numerous occasions where things we believed to be true turned out to be false. We have incorrectly embraced mistaken ideas in the past, and it is likely that some of our current beliefs are incorrect as well. This probably doesn't alarm us too much; after all, we expect to make mistakes, and we all recognize that we are susceptible to errors in judgment. Given the sheer volume of what we know, it is to be expected that at least a few of our assumptions are inaccurate.

Critical thinkers endeavor to uncover the truth about information. We strive to consider both sides of a debate, examining all claims with intellectual caution. And we are willing to change our beliefs and adopt new attitudes when the evidence supports a different truth than the one we originally defended. Truth as a concept is relatively simple: Something is true if it agrees with the actual state of affairs in the real world. If we believe that we weigh less than 150 pounds, but an accurate scale shows a weight of 165, then the truth is that we weigh more than 150, and we are mistaken to believe otherwise. However, it is not always easy to gauge the truth of statements, ideas, and concepts. Many argue that because opinions vary on different topics, we can never know the actual truth about an idea: What might be true for others might not be true for us. Opinions do differ, and beliefs are subject to error. However, truth is not a concept that holds just for some and not for others. Saying something is true is very much different than saying something is "true to me." It may be fuzzy, indistinct, or difficult to discern, but truth reflects reality, the actual state of affairs as they exist. Although we may not be able to ascertain with total certainty whether something is true, that does not mean that truth does not exist or that continued diligence might not move us closer to knowing the actual state of affairs. Truth is not dependent on whether we believe in it but rather represents the way the world really is. Critical thinking requires that we discard our previous opinions and believe in a state of affairs shown to be true, regardless of whether the new information supports our cherished and deeply held beliefs.

Each of us has a belief structure that contains a surprisingly large array of beliefs. Most of what we assume to be true is derived from this underlying belief structure. However, our belief structure, while relatively consistent, is not static and unchanging. We live in an age of information and are overwhelmed with reports, figures, and data; and our beliefs are undergoing constant revision and updating as we receive new information. With such an abundance of information bombarding us, we selectively direct our attention to incoming facts to decide whether to alter our beliefs or reject what we've heard and retain our established ideas. The way we deal with this barrage of incoming news is determined in large part by what we already believe (Rudinow & Barry, 1994). Much of this process involves protecting and defending what we currently know because we tend to assume our own beliefs are likely superior to contrary beliefs—views that threaten our strongly held convictions are seldom given thorough consideration. In fact, we tend to reinforce our attitudes by avoiding material presenting opposing views. Those with particularly strong attitudes toward a given subject (such as religion or politics) would be unlikely to actively seek out incompatible information and ideas. Critical thinkers actively seek to examine their own belief structures and test these assumptions to assure accuracy.

We have attitudes toward everything, from political figures to vegetables to the people at work. But how do we develop our attitudes? Attitudes (Rosenberg & Hovland, 1960) comprise our emotional reactions (how we feel about something), our beliefs (what we think about something), and our behaviors (how we act toward something). Our attitude toward the mayor might be that we like her as a person, we believe she is honest and hardworking, and we plan to vote for her during the next election. Similarly, our attitude toward our boss would include our feelings toward him, the beliefs and knowledge about him that we have acquired, and our inclination to act in certain ways toward him. The intensity or strength of the attitudes we hold determines to a large extent our willingness or openness to altering our viewpoint. For example, if an employee holds a core value that invasion of privacy is bad (a belief) and that random drug testing at work invades privacy, then she is likely to have strong feelings (an emotion) on the subject and would likely react negatively (a behavior) to a proposal to introduce random substance-abuse testing on the job. And we would also expect her to be less susceptible to persuasive arguments about possible benefits from a drug-testing program than a worker with a less intense attitude.

The beliefs and attitudes we possess come from a variety of sources. The most straightforward origin of attitudes is direct experience, and attitudes developed through experience tend to be the most difficult to reject or change (Fazio & Zanna, 1978). Familiar adages such as "seeing is believing" and "experience is the best teacher" exemplify the importance of experience in forming and maintaining our attitudes. If you rent a Ford Taurus on your vacation and experience mechanical difficulties that strand you for 2 days in a small town, you will likely have a negative attitude toward the car (and possibly the manufacturer) regardless of how highly the Taurus is rated by *Consumer Reports* and your friends who own one. Similarly, an employee who experiences difficulty working for a particular woman may develop an attitude that women in general do not make good managers. Contrary evidence carries little weight when it conflicts with what we have personally experienced.

In addition to experience, we also develop attitudes through exposure. Exposure is one of the reasons why advertisers spend so much money to run their commercials over and over until consumers become familiar with their product and name. Repeated exposure to a specific source often leads to positive attitudes even when we are unaware of such exposure (Moreland & Zajonc, 1979). Over time, we tend to like what we recognize. When personal computers first became available, many businesses reacted indifferently (or even negatively). Computers were often seen as expensive toys that added little benefit to the bottom line. However, an office without a computer looks out of place today. As exposure increased and more and more offices adopted the new technology, business attitudes shifted from indifference to overwhelming acceptance.

Our attitude toward an object can be influenced by how information is presented to us. For example, presenting opposing sides of a controversial issue can be more persuasive and influential than attempting to persuade solely from a favored position (McGuire, 1964). Presenting information about both sides of a complex issue to an informed and skeptical audience tends to be more credible because skeptics can appraise the merits of the situation along separate, independent dimensions (Swinyard, 1982). Furthermore, persuasion tends to be more successful if the source is seen as expert, trustworthy, and attractive (Cooper & Croyle, 1984). The choice of words used (such as the euphemisms in Table 6.1) to present ideas also influences attitudes toward the topic. Politicians and marketers attempt to sway public opinion by using words such as *quarantine* for naval blockade, *police action* for war, *tabloid* for newspaper, and so on. Or consider a candy bar with the words "BIGGEST EVER!" printed on the wrapper. Although the implication is that the candy is larger than before, the actuality is that the bar is as big as it always was: It hasn't changed size.

Attitudes and beliefs give us our frame of reference and establish our worldview. We rely on this belief structure to interpret new experiences and guide our behavior (Rudinow & Barry, 1994). When we are exposed to new information, we use our frame of reference to determine whether new data will be incorporated into our existing beliefs, modified to fit with what we already know, or rejected outright. Our thinking and judgment are mediated by the attitudes we hold. Personal beliefs and attitudes can and do influence our decisions, and critical thinkers need to be aware of whether their conclusions are based either in whole or in part on personal opinion rather than objective knowledge. Critical thinking requires reflective skepticism, a cautionary approach that demands reasonable (as opposed to absolute) supportive evidence before we willingly believe arguments and claims and change our belief structure (Brookfield, 1987).

The application of critical thinking skills requires us to be both imaginative and disciplined. We are encouraged to be open (but skeptical) to new ideas, new concepts, and new ways of doing things. Even if alternative explanations fail to conform to our preconceptions of reality, we need to look at them objectively and see if they fit the facts as we understand them. Critical thinking is two-pronged: It requires that we openly consider possibilities, even the far-fetched and unlikely, and it requires that we skeptically scrutinize everything, both novel ideas and established wisdom. Those concepts that pass the test, that mesh with our internal standard of acceptability, become beliefs, whereas those that fail are discarded. As we consider whether to accept fresh information and form new beliefs,

TABLE 6.1 **Examples of Euphemisms**

Euphemism	*Meaning*
Downsizing	Firing employees
Negative profits	Losses
Terminal living	Dying
Gather intelligence	Spy
Terminate	Kill
Strategic withdrawal	Retreat
Operation Just Cause	Panama invasion
Operation Desert Storm	Iraq invasion
Sanitize	Destroy

SOURCE: Lutz, W.(1989). *Doublespeak: From "revenue enhancement" to "terminal living"—How government, business, advertisers, and others use language to deceive you.* New York: Harper & Row.

the question of acceptance boils down to one main point: How good is the evidence?

In the computer-purchasing example cited earlier, we found that opinions varied as to which brand would best suit our needs. In fact, according to the sales literature of the different manufacturers, every computer maker believes (and attempts to persuade us to agree) that its line is superior to the competition (at least on those features that are truly important). How do we determine the extent to which the various claims are true? To confirm the facts and weigh the evidence, we will need to consider the source, generate alternative explanations, and test what we believe.

CONSIDERING THE SOURCE

Critical thinking requires that we confirm the facts available to us to determine how likely they are to be correct. So how do we know if the facts we are told are true? And for the facts we have already accepted as valid, how did we arrive at the conclusion that they were worthy of belief and adoption? The most important single element that determines the extent to which we believe an item of information is true (and therefore worthy of becoming our own opinion or belief) is the source of the fact. Would you be more likely to believe an article in the *National Enquirer* or in the

New York Times? The confidence we give the information we receive (deciding whether facts are likely to be valid) is directly related to our estimation of the credibility of the source.

Ultimately, all of what we know to be true (everything we believe) derives from the authority we bestow on the source of that belief. Most of our perceptions of the truth of the world come from an authority figure (an expert), someone who knows substantially more about the authenticity of the topic (or so we believe) than we do; however, some of our beliefs are self-generated—we came up with them ourselves (in a sense, we are our own authority figure). Authority figures can be individuals (such as a parent, teacher, doctor, or priest) or groups (such as the government, the media, a corporation, the American Medical Association, and so on), and most of what we claim to know comes from them. We rely on authority figures for facts and opinions about history (and the cosmos) and the health of the economy (or our own health), about what happened today in the neighborhood (or around the world), and about our religious beliefs (or lack thereof), the correctness of social action (how to behave around others), and an almost limitless list of additional topics that form our conception of reality. Sometimes, we develop our own beliefs rather than accepting an outside reference: We become our own source of authority. Our self-generated truths may develop due to intuition ("It just feels right"), direct experience ("I've seen it with my own eyes, regardless of what they say"), or faith (belief that does not rest on logical proof or material evidence), but they carry as much weight as truths from external authority figures.

Authority figures have a tremendous impact on what we know and accept. Credible sources of authority can impress, influence, and intimidate to an extent that we abandon our previously held beliefs and judgments. For example, one source of authority is what others consider to be true: We assume the majority view is most likely to be correct, and when our judgment differs from what most people believe, we frequently change our belief to match the majority opinion (Asch, 1956). So if almost everyone at the staff meeting is in favor of a questionable proposal, we are much more likely to reevaluate our belief and adjust it to be more in line with the will of the majority (Janis, 1982). Whether doing so stems from majority opinion or some other source, it makes sense to rely on external authority much of the time. We simply cannot test and explore all possibilities ourselves, nor can we become experts in every field of knowledge. Although we have compelling reasons to rely on reliable authority figures, our judgments of what is true must still derive from the weight of the evidence presented to support a given claim.

We can likely accept the assertions of authority figures if the person (or group) is recognized as an expert in the field, when an authority is trustworthy, when other authorities (in general) are in agreement with the espoused view, and if we have the capability (at least potentially) of testing claims to determine if they are correct. If the Surgeon General states that smoking is harmful and causes cancer, you would likely have legitimate cause to accept his claim as true. Your judgment of his opinion would be based on his recognized expertise in the field of medicine, the likelihood that the Surgeon General is honest (in the absence of contradictory evidence), the general agreement from other sources (except from tobacco manufacturers) that cigarettes are indeed harmful, and your access to studies that scientifically support his claims (and even the theoretical possibility of performing experiments yourself). So, for example, if you need to decide which computers will best serve your departmental needs and the various credible experts you consult support a particular model, your confidence in the correctness of your choice increases substantially. However, in spite of the inherent plausibility of a given authority figure, we need to be aware of possible biases in our assessment of the truthfulness of information when we rely on authority.

Many times, we assign too much weight to an authority figure's view because we perceive the authority source to be infallible. However, even the most knowledgeable experts are susceptible to mistakes (Gazzaniga, 1985). So although a source of new information has been faultless in the past, we cannot allow an authority figure to be invincible to skepticism and doubt. For example, previous major decisions made by your boss have turned out great, so you readily accept his assessment of the current problem and his suggested solution. Believing that an expert data source cannot be mistaken can lead to extreme outcomes (witness the many examples of infallible spiritual leaders who have led their followers to personal loss and even death by suicide). In addition, we sometimes give irrelevant or unrelated information supplied by authority figures too much sway over our judgments. An expert with recognized knowledge in one field who provides advice in an unrelated field is typically relying on reputational appeal. So we may allow an acclaimed expert (perhaps the company's technical guru) to have undue influence when she offers her opinion in another arena of expertise. Television ads using endorsements of well-known celebrities are an appeal of this type (as demonstrated by the familiar "I'm not a doctor, but I play one on TV" commercials). While it is possible that an individual who is brilliant in one field may also be well informed and insightful in another, we must be aware of possible biasing if experts attempt to transfer their credibility to another topic.

Much of what we believe to be true comes not from an external source of authority but rather from within. For example, when we base a judgment on instinct or intuition, we are allowing an internal standard to establish the truthfulness of what we know. Instinct and intuition are responses at the emotional level, feelings we have that we can't quite put a finger on. We may accept (or reject) a proposed project, but we are unable to put into words why we feel the way we do. We believe certain things are true because they *should be* true—they possess the aura of plausibility. Emotions are the driving force behind our thought, so intuitive decisions or beliefs that elicit an emotional reaction tend to focus our attention (Sylwester, 1995). Intuitive beliefs driven by emotions are not necessarily incorrect; they are, however, susceptible to biasing influences. Because we are unable to quantify our intuitive beliefs, it becomes very difficult to test their reliability. We are unsure ourselves why we feel the way we do ("It just seems right"), so we are unclear what evidence would be required to disconfirm our beliefs. A further difficulty is separating what we intuitively believe from what we wish to be true. We may have a gut feeling that a relative who is diagnosed with terminal cancer will recover, but the fine line between desperate optimism and genuine belief becomes difficult to distinguish; our actions can convince ourselves as well as others of what we believe (Bem, 1972).

Our self-generated truths may also develop from our personal experiences. Coastal inhabitants and seafarers were among the first to believe the new-fangled "round world" theory (rather than the widely accepted flat-earth theory) due to their personal experiences. Sailors and fisher folk had long recognized that the mast of a returning ship was visible on the horizon well before the ship's body, an experience that matched nicely with the idea of a sphere-shaped world. Conventional wisdom argues that experience is the best teacher of what is true. However, experience as a source of authority is also prone to error. For one thing, experience relies heavily on memory, and human recall is limited and subjective (Simon, 1990). Memories fade with time, and it appears that we actively reconstruct our memories to match our expectations when we remember. We are unable to record all relevant events deriving from experience, and our constrained memories are further colored by our inaccurate recall and application of what we've learned (Loftus, 1980). Memories are constructed at the time of withdrawal, and any missing pieces are filled in (within a split second) with logical inferences, similar memories, and other relevant information. As an example, picture a scene where you experienced something pleasurable. If you are like most people, the scene you envision includes you as an actor, and your brain must have added you to the picture because you were unable to view yourself at the time of the event (Myers, 1990). Experience is based on memory, and memories are often incorrect. Research suggests that up to 90% of what we experience can no longer be recalled within 2 weeks of an event (Hunter, 1964). And even if our memories are accurate, we cannot always trust our own experiences or the evidence of our own eyes. Our experience may have been atypical or highly improbable (although one-in-a-million events are extremely rare, they do happen one in a million times), incorrectly interpreted or misunderstood, or biased by our perceptions (Bruner & Postman, 1949).

Another internalized source of authority is faith (for example, beliefs derived from spiritual teachings such as the Koran, the Bible, the I Ching, and so on). Faith is generally held as an optimal standard of what the world should be like, what we should do, or how things ought to be. Accepting the truthfulness of an idea or fact on faith entails a willingness to believe without the need for empirical or external verification and support. Answers to metaphysical, religious, and abstract philosophical issues are generally supported by an appeal to faith. Issues that appear to be unexplainable by usual means or events outside of objective experience typically rely on faith for support and confirmation. Of course, one of the major difficulties arising from reliance on faith is that it tends to be self-perpetuating. Supportive evidence is not necessary, and in fact, evidence contrary to our faith-supported belief carries no weight and is ignored. For example, creationists who believe the universe is only 6,000 years old are unwilling to consider substantial contradictory biological and geological evidence, as well as radioactive and cosmological facts (for example, stars and heavenly bodies such as the Milky Way that are more than 6,000 light years away should not be detectable because nothing older than 6,000 years exists). Contrary information is incompatible with creationist beliefs, and it is summarily dismissed.

Much of the information we receive every day comes from conversations with friends, acquaintances, and colleagues. Many of us intuitively recognize that some personal contacts pass on consistently more reliable information than others; some sources are more trustworthy and credible. However, regardless of the source of our secondhand data, we need to keep in mind that other humans are subject to the same judgmental and decisional biases as we are, and that much secondhand information can be erroneous (Gilovich, 1987). When events are described to another, the message is almost always tailored to be more understandable and meaningful for the receiver. The essential components of the message need to be conveyed, but we try not to burden others with too much detail. In addition, the human mind is only capable of retaining and using a limited amount of information, further reducing the accuracy of the original data. Typically, when information is passed on orally, speakers tend to sharpen or emphasize what is deemed to be truly important and to level out or deemphasize less essential aspects of the message. The information conveyed tends to be a simplified version of the original, the condensed essence minus detailed embellishment. Although sharpening and leveling of secondhand information eases both its transmittal and reception, inaccuracies and inconsistencies are unavoidable. As an example, try to recall your first meeting with someone who had been vividly and excitedly described to you, either in positive or negative terms ("He's unbelievably mean-spirited and arrogant" or "She is so energetic and charismatic"). When we finally meet this individual, we are invariably disappointed; people are rarely the monsters or deities we are led to believe they are. Secondhand information focuses on the main points the sender deems important as well as on the components assumed to be of interest to the listener. By the same token, messages lose much of their relevant content and become less accurate when passed through increasing numbers of contacts (Allport & Postman, 1947).

CONSIDERING ALTERNATIVE
EXPLANATIONS

Clearly, people (like computer makers) can benefit if they are able to persuade us to accept their particular point of view. This is not to say that persuasive information is wrong or incorrect, just that we need to be aware that several motives may lie behind what we are asked to consider. If others will gain the advantage (by getting us to purchase their product, for example), then they should realistically expect to supply us with reliable evidence to validate their claims. Positive evidence supporting the phenomenon is necessary for us to accept a statement as fact or for us to incorporate a given viewpoint into our belief structure. However, although evidence is required, it is not, by itself, sufficient for us to accept the information as valid or for us to change our minds if alternative explanations exist that account for the facts better. Unfortunately, decision makers often mistakenly accept data that suggests, rather than confirms, a belief to be true. This illusion of validity arises when we fail to realize that a given belief is not a logical conclusion derived from objective evidence but rather a matter of opinion or values (Einhorn & Hogarth, 1977). For example, your company uses a psychological profile (a personality test) to measure the suitability of job applicants (those who score below a certain cutoff point are no longer considered for employment), and the human resources department claims the test is very effective in reducing personnel costs because only 2% of new hires quit within the first year. However, the argument is flawed unless worthy candidates who failed to pass the test are also hired to see if they are more or less likely to quit than those who passed the test. Because those below the cutoff point were never hired, it would be inaccurate to assume that they would have had a higher rate of attrition. The accuracy of the test, although suggested, has not been confirmed.

Critical thinking requires that we engage in active consideration of possible alternative explanations and not take presented evidence at face value. Because the primary purpose of some information such as advertising is to motivate and direct our actions, it is not surprising that facts contained in sources like advertisements are often presented ambiguously to sway consumer opinion. For example, the manufacturers of Profile Bread claimed their product aided weight loss because it contained seven fewer calories than other breads. However, when confronted by the Federal Trade Commission, the Continental Baking Company reluctantly admitted that their bread was sliced thinner than the competition's bread, resulting in the advertised calorie reduction (Rudinow & Barry, 1994). And Ford advertised its LTD automobile as "700% quieter," suggesting that this year's model was seven times quieter than previous models. Ford admitted (when challenged by the FTC) that the basis for their comparison was exterior noise, meaning that sitting in the LTD was 700% quieter than sitting outside (Rudinow & Barry, 1994). When information is being used to persuade us to a particular course of action (such as buying a product), critical thinking requires that we be scrupulous about examining the evidence imparted in persuasive attempts and that we consider alternative explanations to the facts presented to us. Evidence needs to be carefully examined to determine the extent to which facts are presented objectively, neutrally, and without bias. Rather than being passive acquirers of information, we need to question the motivation behind the evidence we hear. Whose interests are being served, what alternate explanations might also be plausible, and does the perspective being offered take us closer to or further from the likely truth?

Once an initial belief about something has been formed, we tend to seek out information that confirms our expectations (Klayman & Ha, 1987). When we're considering candidates for particular positions, we seek information from them that supports what we expect their abilities should be to do the job (Snyder & Cantor, 1979). For example, if we need a salesperson and we believe salespeople should have outgoing personalities, we would seek confirmation that candidates are extroverted. On the other hand, if we are looking for a researcher and we believe researchers are reclusive, we would likely seek information confirming that candidates are shy. We prefer information that is consistent with our anticipation rather than contrary to it.

This tendency toward seeking to confirm our expectations can have far-reaching and long-lasting effects. If we expect the new hire to be a star performer, then we are much more likely to focus on instances when she lived up to our expectations and to overlook or minimize the times when performance was below average. If we believe a certain ethnic group is hard-working (or lazy), we recognize examples that support what we expect and fail to see contrary cases (Word, Zanna, & Cooper, 1974). If we are thinking about starting a new product line, we seek out only data that confirm it will succeed before we commit. And when we seek to test our beliefs, we ask questions and target responses that support our point of view. As an example, consider the following numerical sequence (Wason, 1960):

2, 4, 6

These three numbers conform to a simple rule. Your objective is to uncover that numeric rule by thinking of sets of three numbers that might conform (or not) to the rule. What three-number sets do you consider?

Here are a few number sets that follow the numeric rule: (8, 10, 12), (14, 16, 18), (100, 102, 104), (1000, 1002, 1004), (3110, 3112, 3114), (9888, 9890, 9892). Likely these are similar to what you expected. No surprises so far, right? However, here are some number sets that also follow the numeric rule: (1, 2, 3), (1.6, 9.1, 27.2), (111½, 213¾, 731¼), (−41, −37, −2). The rule for the first three figures in the problem above was *three numbers in increasing order of magnitude,* so any three ascending numbers would be correct number sets. Many of us have seen similar number problems and set our expectations accordingly. When first viewed, most people anticipate that the number rule is likely to be *ascending even numbers,* so they imagine number sets that are divisible by two. Because our belief is that the number set is three ascending even numbers, we seek information that confirms our expectations. However, notice that if we believe the numeric rule to be ascending even numbers and we continue to list only sets where the numbers go up by two, we will never get to the "true" rule. For each set of ascending even numbers we list, we would get confirmation that it fits the facts, but our interpretation of the facts would be wrong. It is only when we seek to disconfirm what we believe that we generate truly useful information. If we believe the rule is ascending even numbers and list 1, 3, 5, we might expect that the number set would not fit. If, in fact, we found that 1, 3, 5 failed to conform, we would gain support for our initial expectations—because 1, 3, 5 are not even numbers, and if the set did not conform, we would receive more support than listing all the possible even-numbered sets. However, we also gain useful information when we fail to disconfirm. If we list 1, 3, 5 with the expectation that it will not fit and then discover that it does conform, we need to reevaluate our hypothesis and derive a rule where the evidence fits the facts. Disconfirming what we believe to be true usually gets us closer to the true answer (Russo & Schoemaker, 1989).

Research indicates that people are geared toward seeking to confirm their hypotheses (Snyder & Cantor, 1979). As an example, if we are asked whether our friend Jane would be better suited for an outgoing job like a real estate salesperson or an introverted job like a research librarian, we tend to ask ourselves what we know about Jane's past history that supports our belief about her suitability for a particular job. If we believe Jane might make a good real estate salesperson, we would attempt to retrieve from memory instances when Jane acted in an outgoing manner suitable for our expectations of a sales position, such as when she socialized with neighbors. However, if we have a sufficient store of information about Jane, it is also likely that we would be able to recall situations that support the opposite hypothesis as well, such as times when Jane avoided meeting new people. Knowledge of our preference for seeking confirming evidence to support our expectations enables us to be aware of potential judgmental bias. Because supportive evidence to confirm contrary positions (such as whether Jane should become a salesperson or librarian) is readily retrievable from memory, we generally benefit from attempting to find examples that disconfirm what we expect to uncover. We may find that although we initially believed Jane would make a good real estate salesperson, we generated many more examples of her acting shy and withdrawn when we attempted to disconfirm our initial impression, suggesting that she might make a better librarian instead.

To overcome our tendency to seek out and interpret information that confirms established beliefs, we need to be aware that the confirmation bias is a strong psychological force. We may not even be aware that we have prejudged a problem and arrived at a solution until after our decision has been made. Confirmation seeking often works at a subconscious level. Also, human nature drives us toward things we like and away from things we dislike. We like a certain point of view because we are already leaning that way, and we are attracted to evidence and information that supports what we like and leads us to believe that our initial beliefs were well-founded and justified. We can minimize our tendency toward confirmation by forcing ourselves to play devil's advocate: Why shouldn't we do the opposite? What's a good reason to do something else? Furthermore, we need to make an effort to seek out conflicting evidence. Finally, it helps to seek out information from others, but we must be careful about asking leading questions that invite confirmation of what we already believe.

This tendency we possess of expecting things to conform to our beliefs can lead to a self-fulfilling outcome. The possibility of self-fulfillment has also been called the Pygmalion effect (Rosenthal, 1987). According to Greek myth, Pygmalion was an artist who sculpted a feminine statue of such great beauty that he fell in love with his own creation and wished that it might live. The goddess of love took pity on the love-struck sculptor, brought the statue to life, and Pygmalion's expectations came true. The

Pygmalion effect suggests that if we expect something to happen, our expectations and the way we act can cause the anticipated effect. As an example, your belief that an employee is generally hostile causes you to be unfriendly and defensive toward him, and your actions bring about the anticipated hostility. On the other hand, if we expect a new employee will be a pleasant and industrious addition to our department, we are likely to be friendly and helpful toward him, behaviors that assist his ability to be pleasant and industrious. Unfortunately, negative self-fulfilling prophesies are probably more likely to come true (Nisbett & Smith, 1989). If we expect an employee to be incompetent, we will likely never give her the opportunity to prove otherwise by assigning her a difficult task, and the absence of positive outcomes is presumed to be confirmation of lack of ability.

TESTING THE FACTS

Critical thinking encourages us to be open to possibilities, but it requires us to be skeptical of any information before we embrace it and adopt it as our own. If we are presented with information that contradicts the experiences and beliefs we've acquired throughout our lives, it is perfectly reasonable to be skeptical of the truthfulness of these opposing facts. Some information is unworthy of in-depth consideration and contemplation. When presented with facts that go against well-established findings, the burden of proof rests with those who claim to have found the new truth. However, skepticism does not equate to closed-mindedness. The scientific community rightfully met stories of cold fusion (the belief that a nuclear reaction that normally requires millions of degrees can occur at room temperature) with extreme skepticism. Even though the prospect seemed far-fetched, some researchers attempted to repeat the procedures that supposedly resulted in cold fusion (with a notable lack of success). Skeptical inquiry refuted the claims, while closed-mindedness would have simply dismissed the idea outright. We are justified in treating implausible and unsubstantiated information with extreme skepticism. We need not feel overly guilty for dismissing out of hand offerings that promise us something for nothing or that ask us to believe based solely on faith.

In the tobacco example cited above, cigarette makers admitted a relationship between smoking and cancer: We often find the second when we find the first. Things are said to be correlated if they vary together: When one increases, so does the other, or when one rises, the other falls. Although many correlated events we witness are causal (one causes the other to occur), many are not. Flipping the light switch and seeing the lamp come on are almost perfectly correlated (the only times turning on the lamp might not result in illumination would be if the bulb were burnt out or if some other event interrupted electrical flow); one does cause the other. But some things that vary together are not related. For example, when ice cream sales increase, so do reported drownings. While it might be true that consuming ice cream causes people to drown (perhaps parental advice against swimming after eating was correct after all), a much more likely explanation is that some other factor or event is causing them both. In this example, the most likely cause would be temperature: As the weather warms, we tend to eat more ice cream, and we also tend to swim more than in cooler months.

Most of the time, when we witness two events varying together (when things are correlated), they are also causally connected: One makes the other occur. Rain does generally result from increasing cloudiness (and we rarely find rain when clouds are absent), and we do tend to perform better on tests if we study more. The highly organized human brain seeks out patterns and order in all we do, and most of the time when the mind recognizes a relationship (detects a correlation), cause and effect are present. We use correlation quite successfully in our lives to understand why events seem to vary together. We learn quickly not to request favors from the boss during quarterly budgeting time because we've witnessed how infrequently favors have been granted in the past. We understand why (and even come to expect that) we always gain weight during the holidays. Some of the greatest scientific findings have come about due to observed correlation between events (such as the discovery of penicillin). However, correlation does not always mean causality. For example, South Seas natives believe that body lice promote good health because almost all healthy natives have some body lice whereas almost all ill natives do not. Despite this correlation, body lice do not cause healthiness. Instead, lice tend to abandon us when our body temperatures are too high (as when natives are sick), so the actual relationship is that sick natives have fewer body lice (Giere, 1997). And sometimes, one event can cause another without any perceived correlation. Sherlock Holmes solved the mystery of the evening intruder by noticing the curious incident of the dog in the night. When it was remarked that the dog did nothing, Holmes responded that the failure of the dog to bark was the curious incident, noting that the hound must have known the intruder (Nisbett & Ross, 1980). Similarly, sometimes, the cause is distantly related to the event, such as in the connection between smoking and cancer. The cause is present, but the outcomes don't appear until much later.

Suppose you noticed that on certain bright days, workers in the factory appear to perform better; you believe a correlation exists between worker output and lighting intensity. This sounds like a reasonable association, but how would you go about confirming your expectations? One way to find out would be to vary workroom lighting and measure worker productivity. If workers produced more under conditions of better lighting, then you likely have justification for your assertion. Not surprisingly, this very question was tested several decades back during a rather famous series of experiments (Roethlisberger & Dickson, 1939). And as your observed correlation suggested, when experimenters raised illumination levels, they found that workers produced more. Furthermore, when illumination was raised yet again, productivity improved once more. Obviously, better lighting caused better output, right? Although this connection seems clear, is it possible that something else could have resulted in the productivity gains that were observed? How could we find out? If brighter lights caused increased output, then the opposite should be true. So one way to test our findings might be to lower lighting levels and see if performance also declined, which is just what the researchers did. However, contrary to their expectations, the experimenters found that when lighting levels were returned to normal conditions, workers produced even more than they did under bright lights. In fact, productivity continued to improve as lighting intensity was decreased, even when workers were experiencing levels close to moonlight. Obviously, something other than lighting was influencing performance. In this case, debriefing with employees revealed that the mere fact that they were part of an important experiment (a phenomenon that came to be known as the Hawthorne effect) caused the workers to feel special and motivated them to exert extra effort. So although your theory that higher illumination causes better performance might indeed be true, the results of this experiment failed to confirm your beliefs.

Critical analysis is necessary to determine if correlated events are truly cause and effect (Crocker, 1981). When judging what may be applicable to our observed correlation, we need to decide what kind(s) of information will be considered relevant. In the example above, will we only examine cases where lighting is increased, or will we consider instances where illumination is lowered? Will we restrict our considerations just to this factory or include different workers, nonwork conditions, and other situations? Then, we need to collect data (randomly, if possible) from the sources we've deemed appropriate. Here's where we would go out in the plant and monkey with the lighting. Once we've made our observations, we need to interpret and classify them. What will we accept as an increase in performance? How much variation in lighting is required to count as being brighter (or dimmer)? Using our classifications, we need to analyze them by using whatever methods we feel are appropriate. We may simply use a frequency count, or it may be desirable to perform more advanced statistical analyses to measure significance. Finally, we need to use the results of our analysis to make a judgment as to whether the correlation we observed is truly cause and effect. If this seems like a lot of activity, you can see why we prefer to take shortcuts in our decision making. Critical analysis is hard work, and the limitations of human memory as well as likely judgmental biases complicate the task. However, incorrect conclusions may be drawn without critical thinking, making it well worth the effort.

Although a correlation may exist, we have to be careful about the conclusions we draw from correlational relationships. For instance, it is true that most driving deaths occur within 25 miles of home: The likelihood of being in an accident is correlated to the distance we are from where we live (Chandler, 1948). However, this does not mean that the farther we drive from home, the safer we become. Instead, this relationship shows that we do most of our driving near home, and we are, therefore, more likely to be involved in an accident closer to where we live. Similarly, we might read a survey indicating that 94% of chief executive officers (CEOs) possessed a dog or cat when they were young, indicating that pet ownership might develop the character and skills needed to become a successful executive. Although the correlation might be true, it fails to take into account the percentage of non-CEOs who also owned pets as children. If 94% of all children cared for a pet at some time, then the application of the statistic to executives becomes meaningless.

When testing the facts, critical thinkers should search for both supportive and disconfirming evidence. Although both types of evidence are useful, disconfirming evidence carries more weight than supportive evidence (Russo & Schoemaker, 1989). As an example, suppose we are thinking about purchasing a used car. The car salesman assures us that although the automobile we are considering shows excessive mileage on the odometer, we need not worry because the engine is a new replacement. If the salesman is correct, we might expect that the exterior of the motor should look like a new engine, with fresh paint, unworn belts, and no lubrication leaks; and sure enough, the motor looks sparkling clean and new. However, we would also expect that the cylinder compression of a new engine would be significantly higher than that of a worn and tired motor. If we take the vehicle to a certified mechanic to perform a compression test and find that the engine has the low compression we might expect from a used motor, then we have convincing evidence disconfirming the salesman's assertions. A diligent search that fails to find disconfirming evidence is a form of indirect confirmation.

When people are attempting to persuade us to their way of thinking (to purchase their product, for example) or want us to support their belief system, remember that the burden of proof lies with the party presenting the new concept. When a claim is disputed or when information fails to conform to the facts currently in our possession, the producers or purveyors of the new information bear the responsibility of proving the validity of their stand. It is their burden to present us with good evidence that supports their claims, and like a jury, we evaluate what they provide. If the evidence fails to convince us that they are right, then we can safely conclude that at least for now we remain unconvinced until stronger evidence comes to light.

Often, presenters attempt to shift the burden of proof to the audience by challenging us to prove their perspective is invalid or incorrect. The rationale behind this kind of tactic is that if we cannot prove them wrong, then we must agree that they are right. However, failure to find evidence *against* a particular point of view is not the same as finding evidence *for* that point of view. It is not our job to prove their ideas wrong, but rather their job to demonstrate the truthfulness of what they believe. An inability to prove that something is incorrect is not the same thing as evidence proving it is true. The argument that ghosts must be real because their existence has never been disproved does not present evidence to endorse claims of spiritual beings; rather, it is treating the absence of evidence against as proof of supporting evidence. Absence of evidence is not evidence of absence.

In a similar fashion, evidence can be presented in such a way as to lead us to infer desired conclusions. "Has the new employee been caught stealing yet?" suggests that theft is occurring and discovery is just a matter of time. Although this may be the case (the new employee might be stealing), no defensible evidence has been supplied, and the speaker is encouraging us to draw our own unwarranted conclusions. Consider the following:

> Captain L had a first mate who was at times addicted to the use of strong drink, and occasionally, as the slang has it, "got full." The ship was lying in port in China, and the mate had been on shore and had there indulged rather freely in some of the vile compounds common in Chinese ports. He came on board, "drunk as a lord," and thought he had a mortgage on the whole world. The captain, who rarely ever touched liquor himself, was greatly disturbed by the disgraceful conduct of his officer, particularly as the crew had all observed his condition. One of the duties of the first officer (the first mate) is to write up the log each day, but as that worthy was not able to do it, the captain made the proper entry, but added: "The mate was drunk all day." The ship left port the next day and the mate got "sobered off." He attended to his writing at the proper time, but was appalled when he saw what the captain had done. He went back on deck, and soon after the following colloquy took place:
>   "Cap'n, why did you write in the log yesterday that I was drunk all day?"
>   "It was true, wasn't it?"
>   "Yes, but what will the shipowners say if they see it? It will hurt me with them."
>   But the mate could get nothing more from the Captain than, "It was true, wasn't it?"
>   The next day, when the Captain was examining the book, he found at the bottom of the mate's entry of observation, course, winds, and tides:
>   "The captain was sober all day." (Trow, 1905, pp. 14-15)

Although the first mate stated the truth, he suggested from his statement that the captain's sober condition was unusual enough to warrant recording in the ship's log. The evidence presented is true (the captain was indeed sober), but the statement implies a much different (and unsupported) state of affairs.

Facts can be accurate but misleading. It is a fact that more people die in hospitals than anywhere else, suggesting that hospitals are dangerous places to be for those of us who wish to go on living. Perhaps, it is because doctors are incompetent (we have all heard about surgical mistakes where a healthy limb or organ was removed accidentally), conditions are unsanitary (what with all the germs and sick people), or nurses are so overworked that patients don't receive the care they need to survive. Although the preceding are possibilities, it is much more plausible to believe that more people die in hospitals simply because hospitals are where sick and injured people are likely to end up, and the more serious the condition, the more likely the patient is to die. After all, where else would we rather be taken after a car crash?

On August 22, 1989, the *New York Times* reported that "the experts have also developed startling evidence of the cat's renowned ability to survive . . . in New York City where cats are prone at this time of year to fall from open windows in tall buildings" (p. 21). The article goes on to state that 132 cats had been admitted to the Animal Medical Center after having fallen from 2 to 32 stories. Most of the cats had landed on concrete, and most had survived. The article then offers explanations on why cats that fell the farthest were the most likely to live. Primary among the theories under consideration was that when a falling cat reaches terminal velocity, cats may relax and stretch out their legs like a flying squirrel, increasing air resistance and helping to distribute the impact more evenly. A consultant used the article to highlight that of the 22 cats falling more than 7 stories, 21 survived, and of the 13 falling more than 9 stories, all survived, suggesting that falling from a greater height is safer for a plummeting cat than falling from a lesser height. However, the consultant received a letter from a reader telling how the reader's two cats had fallen from her apartment terraces, one from 10 stories and one from 14, how both felines had died, and how the reader had never reported the deaths to the Animal Medical Center (vos Savant, 1996). The additional insight provided from considering unreported feline deaths due to falling demonstrates how we may draw incorrect conclusions if we fail to test the facts thoroughly.

When we are confronted by extraordinary claims, we are justified in requiring extraordinary confirmation. Extraordinary claims are those that are controversial (in some cases, even revolutionary), for which favorable evidence appears to be scanty and that tend to be at odds with conventional understanding or intuition. Those who ask us to accept extreme facts should be held to a higher standard: Decisive supportive evidence is required. Given that we are open-minded and willing to think critically, what stance should we take toward those with extraordinary claims? When evidence is almost entirely anecdotal, skeptical disbelief (with a willingness to reconsider with more compelling evidence) is called for. This is not to say that extraordinary events cannot be true, but rather that evidence must be of sufficient strength to overcome the considerable body of knowledge supporting our current way of thinking. Some far-fetched ideas, although unlikely, do not require that we overturn our current belief structure. No compelling evidence has been presented to demonstrate that the Loch Ness monster exists, but our concept of reality would likely not be shattered if convincing evidence was uncovered. Although most of us would probably be surprised (as well as delighted) by such a discovery, the reality of a Loch Ness monster would simply be a new fact, rather than an earth-shaking revelation. If we saw the Loch Ness monster with our own eyes, that would probably be compelling enough for us to believe. However, if we were to witness someone levitating (which contradicts well-established physical laws), it is much more likely that what we see is a convincing hoax rather than a scientific impossibility (Dawkins, 1986). If simpler, more conventional explanations are unavailable, then further investigation and consideration are justified.

Testing the facts boils down to a case of relative plausibility. If the information presented to us holds up to skeptical scrutiny, then the claims are more plausible than the alternatives under consideration. Rather than being absolute, the concepts we adopt are more plausible than the others that have been put forth based on our understanding of the facts. We are skeptically willing to consider new information and claims when convincing evidence makes them more plausible than believing otherwise. However, when competing alternatives are equally plausible, we remain unconvinced.

ENHANCING CRITICAL THINKING

To improve our critical thinking, we need to recognize when careful decisional scrutiny is appropriate and to realize that we will have to exert the energy required for the application of the necessary thinking skills. Not all decisions are equal in importance or probable impact on our lives. For example, routine problems are generally well served by the effortless processes we have evolved through constant exposure under similar conditions. More important problems require conscious exertion of mental effort, something most of us would prefer not to do because we would rather not put in the time or effort. However, just like any other skill we acquire, critical thinking can only be developed and improved from deliberate and often intense effort on our part. One of the first applications of critical thinking is making a determination as to where it should be applied. Because critical thinking requires a considerable amount of mental investment, we need to reserve its application for those problems and situations that are worth the effort. To improve our critical thinking abilities, we need to be willing to engage in and continue working on a complex and difficult task, suppress our nature to be impulsive, be flexible and open-minded, be willing to let go of unproductive decisional strategies we have been using, and be aware of the very real social constraints (such as a need for consensus or compromise) that our decisional processes must confront (Halpern, 1998). In short, critical thinking requires a willingness to exert deliberate, effortful, and intense mental effort (Wagner, 1997).

Critical thinking can be enhanced if we work to develop those skills that most directly apply to our thinking processes. Verbal reasoning skills that enable us to recognize and take a stand against persuasive attacks improve our ability to think critically. Understanding and analyzing the components of successful argumentation also improve our critical thinking ability by enabling us to weed out irrelevant information and to uncover unsupported assumptions. In addition, the ability to test proposed hypotheses enables us to determine when assessments are accurate and valid and when scientific conditions such as adequate sample size have been met. And a more complete understanding of probability and uncertainty aids our thinking skills by focusing attention on the likelihood that future or anticipated events will actually come to pass.

Critical thinking is an effortful process. Attitudes that have been shaped over years of personal experience and the habits of the mind we are used to applying are not easily altered. As an example, consider horoscopes. Indications are that the majority of Americans read their horoscopes and believe that the information is so often correct that it must have been written especially for them (Lister, 1992). Does the position of the planets at the time of our birth influence our lives? Why would a horoscope be a valid predictor of someone's future? If we believe in the accuracy of astrological forecasting, are we aware of our underlying attitudes and can we offer clear and explicit reasons to support our beliefs? Is the source of our belief personal (reading a personality description that seems to describe us exactly) or external? Have we considered alternative explanations as to why horoscopes seem to offer accurate personal advice? How might we test the evidence to establish the validity of astrological claims?

A useful critical thinking exercise to determine the truthfulness of horoscopes as valid predictors of personality and the future is to analyze 12 unlabeled horoscopes to select the one that is most descriptive of us and then see if it corresponds to our actual sign. As you might expect, people have difficulty choosing the best description because all seem to contain elements of what we believe about ourselves, and we are just as likely to select any of the offerings as the correct horoscope (Ward & Grasha, 1986). If we were to test the accuracy of various horoscopes, we would likely uncover examples of vague language and fuzzy predictions that might apply to a variety of situations and people. And if we analyze the premise that our time of birth controls our destiny, we would likely be unable to justify and explain why the positions of the planets should have a significant influence on individual human behavior. When we apply critical thinking skills to information at hand, such as the accuracy of astrological predictions, we enable ourselves to make more informed decisions and to solve problems with a greater likelihood of success.

One method suggested as a means to improve critical thinking skills is focusing on the important aspects of a problem and determining what we are required to do with any information we uncover. By asking elaborative questions, we attend to the structural aspects of a problem (Halpern, 1998). Examples of relevant tasks and questions that aid our critical thinking are presented in Table 6.2.

Improved decision making results when we use relevant information to direct and improve our thinking skills. Critical thinking requires that we monitor our thinking processes continually, determine whether sufficient progress is being achieved toward a satisfactory outcome, ensure that we are being thorough and accurate, and allocate our time and mental effort properly (Halpern, 1998). Efficient thinking means we need to be aware of how much time and effort a particular problem is worth so we can determine the proper allocation of these scarce resources. Further-

TABLE 6.2 Examples of Relevant Tasks and Questions

Task/Question	Meaning
Draw a diagram or other graphic display that organizes the information	Makes the structure of the problem clear
What additional information would you want before answering the question?	Requires thinking about what is missing from the information presented
Explain why you selected a particular multiple-choice alternative and why another alternative is second best	Focuses on the thinking that went into an answer rather than the answer itself
State the problem in at least two ways	Determines if a problem is actually many problems with separate solutions
Categorize the findings in a meaningful way	Grouping and labeling may result in the emergence of a previously unrecognized structure
List two solutions for the problem	Encourages creativity
What is wrong with an assertion that was made in the question?	Reminds us that problems often contain misleading information
Present two reasons that support the conclusion and two reasons that do not support the conclusion	Eliminates "black-and-white" reasoning
Identify the type of persuasive technique that is used in the question and whether it is valid or misleading	Considers motives and credibility of information source
What two actions would you take to improve the design of a study that was described?	Illustrates possible types of evidence that might produce different results

SOURCE: Halpern, 1998.

more, we need to determine if the probable outcome resulting from our critical thinking application is worth an extended and careful examination of the problem. Are we moving toward a solution, and can we measure our progress? In short, is this the proper time and situation to use critical thinking?

SUMMARY AND REVIEW

Critical thinking requires that we be open-minded to new ideas and concepts, yet skeptical of everything we hear and believe. Thinking critically means that we are seeking to uncover the truthfulness of evidence presented to us, to determine whether the information agrees with affairs in the real world. Our framework of relatively stable feelings toward people, objects, or ideas (our attitudes and beliefs) guides our behavior and allows us to filter new experiences and information. When examining the evidence, we consider the source of the information to determine the trustworthiness and credibility of what we hear. As we think critically, we consider alternative explanations that might be simpler, more objective, or more plausible. To the extent possible, we test the facts to determine if the evidence can be confirmed or disconfirmed.

Part III

Understanding and Improving Creativity

7 | Thinking Creatively

I n many ways, creativity is similar to humor. To see how, keep track of your thought patterns as you read the following amusing account.

> A young business graduate hired by a supermarket reported for his first day of work. The manager greeted him with a warm handshake and a smile, gave him a broom, and said, "Your first job will be to sweep out the store." "But I have a business degree," the young man replied indignantly. "Oh, I'm sorry. I didn't know that," said the manager. "Here, give me the broom—I'll show you how."

What was it about this event that made it funny? Notice that the last sentence, the punch line, leads the reader in a surprising direction. The college graduate emphasizes his expertise and training, but the store manager reacts as though the young man's comments mean he doesn't know how to sweep. The same phrase ("I have a business degree") suggests different things to the parties involved. This twist in the outcome we anticipate is similar to what occurs in the process of creativity. As in humorous situations that bring us to sudden understanding, creative problem solving leads us to new and unexpected solutions. Creativity is the "ah-ha" response, the lightbulb clicking on, or the sudden insight (*Eureka* means "I have found it!") that brings things together. Similarly, we find humor in situations that surprise us, bring unanticipated insight, or twist our perceptions and expectations. Read the following and see if you find it amusing because of unexpected understanding.

In the men's room at work, the Boss had placed a sign directly above the sink. It had a single word on it—*Think!* The next day, when he went to the men's room, he looked at the sign and right below, immediately above the soap dispenser, someone had carefully lettered another sign which read—*Thoap!*

Again, we find stories like the one above humorous because of our sudden revelation: the unexpected understanding that *thoap* is *soap* pronounced with a lisp. Our ability to see things differently allows us to see the humor in a given situation, and it allows us to uncover creative solutions to the problems we encounter.

Creativity is the production of novel, valuable, relevant, and useful ideas (Amabile, 1988), and creativity may involve meaningfully recombining existing ways (Oldham & Cummings, 1996) or doing something for the first time anywhere by creating something entirely new (Woodman, Sawyer, & Griffin, 1993). To understand this process, we need to examine the factors that contribute to our own creativity. All of us know people with high creative talent: scientists, artists, writers, performers, poets, inventors, and so on. Why is it that some people seem to possess more creative ability than others? Think back on a time when you expressed creativity and compare it to a time when creativity was absent. Why are we sometimes more creative than at other times? As shown in Figure 7.1, research suggests that creativity results from an intersection of the personal resources available to the decision maker during problem solving, the techniques and processes used by the problem solver, and the amount of drive or motivation inherent in a specific problem-solving situation (Amabile, 1988).

PERSONAL CHARACTERISTICS
AND CREATIVITY

Resources. One factor influencing creativity is the personal resources we are able to bring to bear: the amount of knowledge, expertise, and technical information available to us as decision makers (Woodman et al., 1993). The facts, skills, and talents we have in place set the stage for the entire range of possible responses we might generate to a specific problem. Previous experience and learning set in motion the pathways we use for solving a particular kind of problem. Some of our expertise and knowledge results in common, well-practiced, or obvious ways of think-

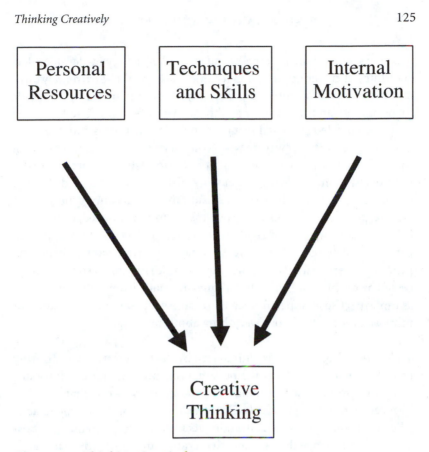

Figure 7.1. Thinking Creatively

ing about a problem (Amabile, 1988), whereas other skills allow us to conceive of new combinations or approaches to problem solving (Stein, 1989). Our knowledge and expertise provide us with the raw materials needed to generate a creative solution, as well as the information we need to judge the suitability of any creative response. The larger our bank of personal resources, the greater the number of combinations and alternatives we have available to us for generating something new and useful related to the problem at hand. Factual knowledge about aspects of the problem (such as in-depth understanding of principles and expertise within the field) provide decision makers with the building blocks from which creativity arises. For example, a production manager would be incapable of coming up with a creative way of improving manufacturing

processes without an awareness (and most likely a very in-depth understanding) of current production techniques. It would be extremely difficult for us to generate novel and new ways of doing things if we had little
or no understanding of the way things currently work. The larger the
scope of knowledge related to a given field in our possession, the more
material we have to draw from when considering possibilities. This is not
to say that newcomers to a field might not demonstrate greater creativity
than decision makers with longer work histories (often they do). More
experienced and knowledgeable decision makers may not generate creative responses, not because they possess too much knowledge but rather
because they may remain rigid and inflexible in the way they approach
problems (Amabile, 1988). Greater amounts of relevant information
cannot hinder creativity, but the way that information is stored and accessed by problem solvers can. As conventional wisdom often indicates,
as our expertise in a specific area increases, we tend to narrow our focus
until we eventually "know everything about nothing."

Techniques. Creativity is also influenced by the techniques we use during
problem solving. Applying the personal resources we have will usually
result in a problem solution that is "good enough"—one that satisfices
by meeting minimal standards. However, creative solutions tend to arise
when decision makers apply thinking techniques that expand their possibilities and change their perspectives, rather than using the tried-and-
true decisional processes that generally come up with an adequate response. So even problem solvers who are extremely knowledgeable may
not produce creative work if they apply the wrong techniques to resolve
their problems; their responses will be appropriate (possibly even very
good) but not original, new, or exciting. Also, even relatively naïve and
inexperienced people may generate highly creative solutions due to the
techniques they bring to bear on the problem situation; their approaches
to decision making can generate enlightened responses that are novel,
useful, and relevant (Amabile, 1988). Problem-solving techniques that
allow us to break our mental set, that encourage us to look at things differently, and that keep us exploring new options increase the probability
that creativity will result. It is in the area of creativity techniques that
training and practice can enrich our decisional skills; in fact, the overwhelming majority of creativity training efforts succeed in improving
participant problem solving (Treffinger & Gowan, 1971).

Motivation. In addition to personal resources and thinking techniques, one of the strongest influences on individual creativity is internal motivation (Amabile, 1988; Barron & Harrington, 1981; Woodman et al., 1993). Motivation from within (as opposed to an external source of motivation such as a deadline, a bonus, or some type of reward) can have a strong impact on how we think and perform (Williams, 1998). We are internally motivated when we find something interesting, involving, exciting, satisfying, or personally challenging; and even the best personal resources and techniques will not result in inventiveness if the motivation to be creative is absent (Amabile, 1997). Motivation directs our attention (Simon, 1967), and when our motivation arises from outside sources, then creativity can diminish because we focus our attention on meeting external demands. Often, we revert to simpler, well-established thought patterns that satisfy minimum standards rather than seeking creative and exciting solutions. Because we are motivated by something outside the problem itself, we are encouraged to find a safe and comfortable solution rather than wasting time and effort exploring creative possibilities. Motivation makes the difference between how creative people *can* be and how creative they *will* be related to a specific problem (Amabile, 1988). As an example, imagine reading a mystery. The point of a mystery is to uncover the villain: The fun (or the motivation) is puzzling out who the suspects are, what their motives are, and how they are able to perpetrate the crime. The joy of reading a mystery vanishes if we know who the guilty party is before we have an opportunity to solve the mystery ourselves. Our motivation is to discover the answer, but we want to enjoy the process of discovery as we work through the enigma. The interest and challenge of working on the puzzle are motivational. Of course, we eventually want to reach a conclusion (to reveal the criminal), but we enjoy the freedom of being able to prolong the chase and remain within the story. In fact, we are often pleased and thrilled when a mystery takes an unexpected turn or new evidence is uncovered—much as we are when we find creative solutions to our problems. So although knowledge, expertise, and thinking skills provide the ammunition for creative problem solving, motivation determines the extent to which these resources will be used (see Table 7.1).

Although creative people come from varied backgrounds, one thing they all seem to have in common is a love of what they are doing. Interviews with people ranging from engineers and chemists to writers and

TABLE 7.1 Characteristics Required for Creativity

Characteristic	Examples
Resources	Expertise, experience, familiarity, knowledge, technical skills
Techniques	Cognitive style, ability to take new perspectives, applying appropriate thinking skills, energetic approach to problem solving
Motivation	Appropriate rewards (such as recognition and encouragement), clearly defined goals, constructive feedback, challenge, interest, willingness, enthusiasm, freedom to explore, passion for what you are doing

musicians confirm that creative individuals have fun pursuing what they love and enjoy discovering something new in what they do (Csikszentmihalyi, 1997). Creative people appear to be able to achieve a balance, matching their skills and abilities to their opportunities for designing something new and innovative. Distractions become vague, worries about failure disappear, the sense of time urgency vanishes, and they are able to single-mindedly focus their activity toward a creative outcome. Internal motivation or the opportunity to work at something they enjoy doing determines the extent to which creative people fully engage their resources and techniques in the service of creative performance. Furthermore, motivation can to some extent make up for a deficiency of either or both of the other two personal characteristics necessary for creativity (Amabile, 1997). Creativity thrives when we do what we love and love what we do.

Personal resources, thinking techniques, and motivation to perform are all necessary for creativity to occur: The more we have of each, the greater our creativity. Personal resources provide the background support material; thinking skills provide the processes used to sift, combine, and inspect the personal resources we have; and motivation provides the drive to use our resources and techniques to develop the best possible outcome. Creativity suffers if we do not have enough experience or knowledge about the subject at hand, if we apply incorrect analyses to our problem, or if we lack the motivation to develop an optimal solution. However, creativity increases as we bring more of each of these components to bear on our problem solving. Figure 7.2 graphically displays the relationship among the three components of creativity (Amabile, 1988).

THE STAGES OF CREATIVITY

Creative problem solving usually follows a series of steps (Hogarth, 1980; Wallas, 1926). In most cases, creative individuals use a process that, although it does not guarantee a creative outcome, provides the ingredients for developing a creative solution. This five-stage creative model typically includes (a) problem identification, (b) preparation, (c) idea generation, (d) idea validation, and (e) verification. For creativity to occur, all stages in the creative process should be present, and the quality of a creative outcome is primarily determined by the quality of each individual component in the model (Amabile, 1988).

Problem identification. The initial step in creativity is recognizing that a problem exists. As mentioned earlier, decision makers are susceptible to a number of perceptual biases that may lead them either to conclude that the problem is not really a problem or to define the problem incorrectly. To solve a problem creatively, we must first understand the real problem. If we have a productivity issue but identify the difficulty as the need to fire a lazy employee, we have stated the problem in terms of a solution, severely limiting the avenues we might imaginatively consider. Or we may treat the symptom but fail to resolve the underlying cause (as when we solve a leak by using a bucket to catch the drips). Worse yet, we may end up solving the wrong problem. As an example, a well-known story goes that tenants of a 20-floor office building were complaining daily about the slow speed of the single building elevator. When the building manager contacted elevator companies to find out what could be done to "speed up the elevator," he was given a number of options, ranging from installing a new high-speed elevator (very expensive), programming the elevator to stop on alternate floors (forcing some tenants to walk up or down a flight of stairs), or eliminating the top 5 floors from service (again forcing tenants on those levels to walk up from the 15th floor). All of these solutions carried potentially negative outcomes. The manager came up with a creative (and cheap) solution because he redefined the problem from "How do I speed up the elevator?" to "How do I keep tenants from complaining?" His idea? Mirrors were installed in the lobby that enabled waiting people to pass the time and complaints disappeared. Similarly, if you have a flat tire and no jack, your problem isn't "How do I locate a jack?" (which suggests searching for exactly the right

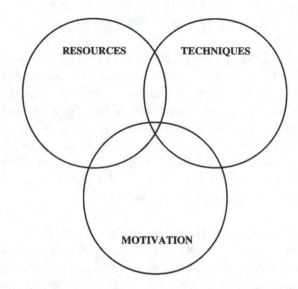

Minimal Overlap Between Resources, Techniques, and Motivation

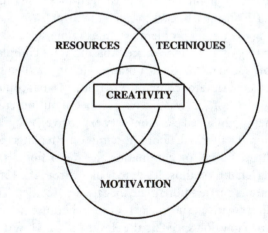

**Major Overlap Between Resources, Techniques, and Motivation
Resulting in High Creativity**

Figure 7.2. Overlap Between Resources, Techniques, and Motivation

tool), but rather "How do I change the tire?" (which suggests that you might be able to use an alternative method to lift the car and remove the tire). It has been argued that few things are as useless as finding the right answer to the wrong question (Drucker, 1954).

Preparation. Once the problem has been properly identified, we need to gather together all the resources necessary to address our concerns. Preparation involves a search for information, clarifying all aspects of the problem, analyzing the resources we can bring to bear, identifying our informational deficiencies, and assessing our assumptions (Bazerman, 1990). If we possess enough knowledge to cope with our problem, then we activate that store of information so it becomes available for use. If we discover that we are deficient in key areas, we can spend time in the preparation stage learning what we need to know (Amabile, 1988). For those whose knowledge base or expertise is sufficient to supply ample approaches and pathways for resolving the problem, this step may be almost instantaneous. However, if needed information is lacking, this stage may be rather long (continuing until we have garnered enough data to move to the following level). Preparation involves understanding, observing, and studying the problem before we turn to resolution.

Idea generation. This is the stage that results in something new or novel. During this phase, decision makers search their knowledge and experience to find relevant information. Here, they sift through what they know and apply various thinking methods to develop ideas and possibilities. The decisional techniques applied determine which pathways or approaches will be explored, the attention devoted to particular aspects of the problem at hand, and the degree to which specific problem-solving procedures will be used to search for solutions (Amabile, 1988). The problem solver's thinking processes also determine how long idea generation will continue and the number of possible solutions to be considered. During idea incubation, we explore unusual possibilities, withhold judgment, probe our assumptions, zero in and elaborate on the problem definition, and contemplate what we know in divergent and flexible ways.

Idea validation. Appraisal of our ideas is suspended until we reach the fourth stage. Here, we evaluate and judge each idea generated during the third phase. Ideas are tested for appropriateness and evaluated for correctness relevant to our knowledge and experience base. True creativity has occurred when we validate that a novel and useful idea is a practical solution to the problem identified in Step 1.

Verification. If the response validated in the fourth stage resolves our problem, the creative process is complete. However, if our idea fails to solve our dilemma, but we appear to be "getting warmer" (Simon, 1978), then we return to Step 1. Based on information gathered during Step 2 (as well as on any learning that occurred during earlier steps), we redefine the problem and continue through the creative process until we return to verification. If we achieve complete failure, then our problem-solving attempts end. However, if a reasonable (but not quite right) response has been developed, the process repeats until we are either satisfied with the outcome or we are convinced that we are unable to generate a creative solution (Amabile, 1988).

The stages of creativity imply a sequential process evolving from recognizing a problem to confirming that our creative output will address it. We observe a situation and, through analysis, attempt to understand the problem and the tools that might be required to resolve it. When we feel sufficiently prepared, we allow our imagination free rein, guiding our mental processes through various channels as we generate novel ideas to meet our specific needs. The ideas we develop are further harvested and enhanced as we validate our thoughts to determine if they are practical and useful. However, our ideas have little value until they are actually implemented and we can verify that our problem has been satisfactorily addressed. When these building blocks of the creative process are properly stacked, novel and practical solutions are often the result.

IMPROVING PROBLEM IDENTIFICATION

One of the most difficult aspects of creative problem solving is ensuring that we have defined the real problem. The time and energy spent on the creative process may produce a new and elegant idea, but that effort will be wasted if the solution fails to resolve the root problem. Therefore, it is critical that we correctly identify a problem before we attempt to tackle it.

To improve problem identification, it helps if we are able to learn as much as we can about the situation. Collecting and analyzing information allows us to sift the important, necessary, and critical data from the irrelevant. Additional information might come from conversations with people familiar with the problem or from viewing the problem firsthand, but regardless of the source of our information, we need to verify our understanding of the problem and all its components (Fogler & LeBlanc, 1995). In addition, it helps us to identify the true problem if we discover where the problem came from (especially if someone else gives us the problem and asks us to solve it), if we distinguish fact from opinion, and if we challenge all assumptions and information presented to us (Kepner & Tregoe, 1981). Although we don't want to ask the question why at this stage, successful problem identification often involves asking who, what, when, and where.

Another technique for improving problem identification is turning the problem around by making the strange familiar and the familiar strange (Gordon, 1961). Purposeful attempts to use metaphors and analogies help to distort and transpose our understanding of the current situation (making the familiar strange). Transforming what we believe into a metaphor or analogy allows us to analyze the out-of-focus problem and develop new insights, which can then be applied to identifying the real problem. For example, if we have identified our problem as low productivity, we might redefine our problem by asking ourselves, "What does this remind me of?" or "What is this like?" We might say that low productivity is like being on a losing sports team or like visiting a dying relative in the hospital. By transferring our problem into something else, we have the opportunity to recognize aspects of something we know quite well (the metaphor) rather than something that feels uncertain (the original problem). New insights can occur because attributes of the redefined problem become evident and can be applied to the original predicament: We are better able to recognize the root problem.

An example of how analogies might be used to develop creative solutions comes from a mining equipment company based in Colorado. A product development team was assigned the task of developing a machine that would both dig and load minerals and ores. An avid bug collector on the team suggested a praying mantis as an analogy: When it eats, it holds its prey between its two extended forelegs. Using the insect analogy, the team came up with a large tractor with a conveyor belt running through two foreleg-like shovels that efficiently load ore (Higgins, 1994).

Problem identification, particularly identification of important problems, can be improved if we include multiple definitions before we proceed to the other steps in the creative process. Formulating more than one definition of the situation allows us to view the same issue from different perspectives, and it may provide us with a greater opportunity to uncover the true problem. Furthermore, if we are able to generate multiple definitions and we phrase our formulation in different terms, we increase the likelihood that we are triangulating toward the real difficulty. For example, if we formulate a problem definition in both human and technical terms, we may see elements of the problem that are not evident in a single phrasing (Mitroff, 1998). We increase the odds that we can zero in on the legitimate dilemma by enlarging and expanding our problem definition. We might ask ourselves if anything else might be included in the problem, if the opposite might be true, or if the problem is part of a larger problem to see if we can identify additional or alternate truths. Likewise, the number of problem definitions can be increased if we try to reverse our problem formulation. Generating contradictions that conceivably could be true simultaneously allows us to look in opposite directions (Rothenburg, 1979) and expands the number of perspectives considered. For example, we might define a productivity problem in terms of employees having too much motivation as well as too little motivation and then analyze the problem from those two positions to see if either helps identify the root cause.

When we identify problems using a linear, straightforward approach, we can be making problem solving more difficult than when we allow ourselves to freewheel and play. Sometimes, creatively identifying the problem can result in a simpler and more efficient route to the answer we are seeking. The traditional method of solving a problem like "What is $\frac{4}{7}$ of $\frac{1}{4}$?" is to multiply the two fractions together to arrive at $\frac{4}{28}$ and then reduce to $\frac{1}{7}$. However, if we describe the problem as "What is $\frac{1}{4}$ of $\frac{4}{7}$?", we are more likely to see that simply taking one fourth of the second numerator results in a quicker solution with fewer steps.

IMPROVING PREPARATION

Often, we move to idea generation before adequately addressing our preparation to proceed (similar to the "ready-fire-aim" approach). We find ourselves attempting to generate possible solutions without sufficient insight or understanding. However, knowledge and expertise play an important role in our ability to be creative (Woodman et al., 1993). Technical skills, talent, experience, and previous learning provide the raw materials needed to generate original and helpful ideas. If we already possess sufficient resources to address the problem, then this store of information is simply reactivated (Amabile, 1988). If adequate resources are lacking, this phase is spent building up the store of information necessary to resolve the problem at hand. For example, getting expertise from others is a good way of overcoming our own lack of knowledge. During the preparation stage, it is not possible for the decision maker to possess too much knowledge (contrary to what many people believe). The amount of information does not inhibit creativity; however, the way that information is stored in memory and the ease with which it is retrieved can have an impact on creativity (Lumsden & Findlay, 1988). Creativity generally suffers if information is stored in rigid, structured patterns (like those used by many experienced thinkers). If memory patterns are flexible, if wide categories of easily accessible information are present, or if particularly appropriate thought processes are made available, creativity can only be increased (Amabile, 1988).

The tools used during preparation (the total amount of experience and knowledge at our disposal) set the stage for how we will view the problem and how we will develop ideas. When compared to novices, experts almost always come up with good (although not necessarily creative) solutions to predictable and routine dilemmas. However, experts are not nearly as successful in solving problems when dealing with inherently unpredictable situations, although their solutions are still generally better than those of newcomers (Shanteau, 1992). In both cases, experts are able to draw from their experience to predict what they can expect from the situation, what differences are reasonable (and how to interpret them), what has typically worked previously, and how historic factors can be shaped to meet current needs. Novices, on the other hand, lack the same store of available information and generally try to follow a cookbook or "paint-by-the-numbers" formula to tackle a problem. Experts more readily recognize meaningful patterns and have in their possession a broader range of tools available to address their concerns. However, if our training and past experience lead us to view a problem from a limited (or even incorrect) perspective, creativity can be stifled. Our very strength (our expertise and knowledge) becomes a deficit because we overconfidently believe we understand the problem, or we wrongly assume the right tools for handling our difficulty include the way we have dealt with similar issues in the past (Amabile, 1988).

Preparation for creativity can be improved if we allow ourselves to pay attention, especially in uncommon ways, to useful concepts derived from the things going on around us. Everyday events can add to our mental storehouse and increase the amount of knowledge available to draw from at a later date (Plsek, 1997). Often, we are able to derive useful information and new insights if we allow ourselves to pause and take notice during our daily activities. By asking ourselves the question, "What is going on at this moment?" we often discover new and useful mental concepts that can be accessed for future problems. Taking a moment to notice and catalog what's going on expands our resources by storing up concepts that might be applicable to a current or future topic. The more information we can retrieve from our mental storage, the more effective the preparation stage becomes. Enhancing our powers of observation and categorization often leads to more creative possibilities.

Preparation involves uncovering what is relevant and necessary for the problem under consideration. Think about the following. You are the driver of a bus, and on the first stop, the bus picks up four people. At the second stop, the bus lets off two and picks up seven more. At the third stop, four people (two with pets) get on, and none leave. At each of the next two stops, three people get on, and one exits. At the final stop, eight people get on while two passengers leave. Now for the question: What color are the bus driver's eyes? Clearly, the most important piece of information needed to prepare for decision making is not the number of stops or the people getting on and off but the preliminary condition stating who the bus driver is. If we have had experience with this kind of puzzle before, the skills are at hand for successful problem resolution. However, if our previous experience with similar situations leads us to believe we are dealing with a quantitative problem, we are likely to use inappropriate methods as we attempt to derive an answer. Although many of the facts in the puzzle seem to be relevant, we cannot apply the appropriate problem-solving strategy until we clarify what tools are needed to proceed.

Preparation is a necessary component of the creative process, and creative preparation can be going on all the time. Expanding our personal resources of information and knowledge increases the amount of useful material available for creative application. Possible tools (Plsek, 1997) that have been found to aid preparation are presented in Table 7.2. Appli-

TABLE 7.2 Tools for Creative Preparation

Tool	*Application*
Pause and notice	• Purposefully set out to notice things or pause when things happen by chance • Assign a meaning to what you see • Don't try too hard • Record your ideas
Take other points of view	• Talk to strangers • Listen intently to others • Try to think like someone else • Even disagreeable or outrageous ideas can be used later • Record your ideas
Refocus a topic	• Explore different statements of the topic • Add structure • Remove structure • Restate key concepts from the topic • Record your ideas
Look closely and analyze	• Ask questions, but avoid answers • Expand your questions as much as possible • Don't overlook the obvious • Seek out patterns
Search for analogies	• Even imperfect analogies can be useful • Focus on common areas between the analogy and the topic at hand • Be literal as well as imaginative • Humor often leads to insight

SOURCE: Plsek, 1997.

cation of some of these tools gives us the storehouse of knowledge that prepares us to take a new perspective and perceive the world in a fresh way.

IMPROVING IDEA GENERATION

At this stage, problem solvers come up with possibilities by searching their knowledge base and using the thinking processes brought forth during the previous phase. Enhanced idea generation occurs if we are flexible in exploring possibilities, are internally motivated to achieve a creative outcome, give attention to particularly relevant aspects of the problem, and follow appropriate thinking processes as we move toward a solution

(Amabile, 1988). Creative problem solvers are those who come up with a broad range of different alternatives rather than a small number of similar concepts. To the extent possible, we need to avoid evaluating (and possibly discarding) ideas as they are developed, we need to encourage ourselves to generate wild ideas (that can be "tightened" later), we should emphasize quantity over quality (at least initially), and we should build on previous concepts (Osborn, 1953). The SCAMPER checklist is often used to enhance idea generation.

- **S**ubstitute by having a person or thing act or serve in place of another as in who else? what else? what other place? and when?
- **C**ombine by bringing together different things such as people, purposes, ideas, materials, and so on.
- **A**dapt by adjusting to suit a purpose or condition by reshaping, tuning, toning, accommodating, and agreeing.
- **M**odify by altering or changing attributes such as form, quality, color, sound, size, and the like. This also includes **M**agnifying and **M**inimizng various attributes.
- **P**ut things to other uses than the original intention, in other places, or at other times.
- **E**liminate some aspects by removing, simplifying, or reducing content.
- **R**everse things by looking at opposites, turning things around, flipping things upside down, or turning things inside out. This also includes **R**earranging the order of various attributes. (Osborn, 1953)

Most of us have difficulty coming up with creative ideas, primarily because we unconsciously impose mental obstacles that constrain the way we look at the problem and that limit the number of alternatives we believe are relevant (Allen, 1974). Rigid, inflexible thinking results from "doing things the right way" rather than taking mental detours, experimenting, and improvising. As an example, if bees (which are fairly logical and analytical for insects) are placed in an open bottle laid on its side with the bottom facing a window, they will persist (until they die of exhaustion or starvation) in trying to go through the bottle's base as they seek escape. However, if flies (which are fairly flighty and feather-brained as insects go) are put in the same bottle, all of them will have found the open exit at the opposite end of the bottle within minutes because of their illogical nature (Sill, 1996). Randomness and paradox can often lead to enlightenment. Some of our most creative ideas are generated when we allow ourselves to be crazy, foolish, and impractical (Von Oech, 1990). By opening ourselves up to new possibilities and change, we are better able to break the rules and explore for ideas in unusual places, generate various imaginative approaches, and use offbeat sources as stepping-stones for more useful and practical ideas. Changing perspectives and playing with what we know enable the mind to transform one thing into another: We can make the ordinary extraordinary and the unusual commonplace. Creative idea generation (Von Oech, 1990) can be improved if we avoid:

Always looking for the "right" answer. Formal education teaches us to seek the correct answer. Throughout our educational lives, we take hundreds of tests that lead us to expect that problems can be solved in only one way; we come to believe that one right answer exists. However, many problems (especially complex issues) can be resolved in more than one way. Creative responses seek to resolve the problem at hand, not to come up with what we believe is the right answer.

Always trying to be logical. Sometimes, our intuition, hunches, and gut reaction can add insight into the creative process. Our remarkable human mind is constantly recording and evaluating information, seeking connections, and storing memories. Disallowing the imaginative input of these factors by always trying to be logical can short-circuit the creative process. Logic drives us to be practical and get the job done. However, creativity requires imagination and a liberal dose of illogic and impracticality.

Strictly following the rules. Again, socialization throughout our childhood has indoctrinated us to be "good" citizens by following the rules. We are encouraged to recite the right answer and discouraged from coloring outside the lines. This tendency to follow the rules means that we often get stuck thinking about things only as they are. Many rules that govern our thinking have outlived their usefulness, so challenging our assumptions and breaking the rules (such as existing policies and procedures) can gain us new perspectives and insights.

Insisting on being practical. Many people have difficulty coming up with creative ideas because they believe their suggestions will be viewed as impractical. Notice that when we present a new concept to others, they generally respond with negatives about what our idea fails to do (all the reasons why it won't work) rather than focusing on the positives that can be used for further improvement. This emphasis on always being practical siphons attention away from the positive, interesting, and potentially useful features of the ideas we develop. Ideas often need to be cultivated and nurtured to produce practical and creative outcomes, but many times, we eliminate good "what if" questions because we seek out only the practical rather than the potential.

Being afraid of failure. Generally, we believe that making mistakes is wrong; error is the same thing as failure. However, most successes result from trial and error, minor modifications of how things are done that improve and correct things. For example, Thomas Edison failed hundreds of times before he perfected the lightbulb, but each mistake got him closer to a creative solution. Failure serves the dual purpose of letting us know what doesn't work and giving us the opportunity to try something else.

Resisting the desire to play. Children and animals play to discover and make sense of the world around them. Playing, as opposed to competing, means that no one wins or loses. Mistakes aren't penalized, but rather we learn from them. As mentioned earlier, humor and creativity use similar processes; having fun and playing can fertilize our thinking.

Becoming too specialized. When we say, "That's not my area," we not only limit the problems we perceive, we also limit the fields of knowledge we bring to the creative process. Categorizing things as within or outside our area not only constrains what we see as problems (or potential problems) but also confines the kinds of knowledge and experience we are likely to apply when generating ideas. By exploring outside our recognized areas, we supply ourselves with additional ammunition and sources of ideas.

Being too concerned with certainty. As mentioned in the section on risk, uncertainty makes us uncomfortable: We strive to control things as much as possible. However, being too specific in our idea generation restricts the range of possibilities open to us. Problems that are clearly stated (with definite and clearly defined boundaries) stifle our imagination. Uncertainty (at least to some degree) allows us flexibility in searching for and playing with ideas.

Not wanting to appear foolish. All of us desire to conform, and we fear doing or saying something that makes us seem foolish. Many imaginative ideas appear to be foolish on the surface, so we are reluctant to share them with others or to give the ideas further consideration. But some problems (or at least the way we are trying to deal with them) cannot be creatively resolved because we are trapped in an unproductive pattern of responses: Our minds are stuck in a rut. When we are stuck in the same old thought patterns, foolishness can often enable us to recognize the habits, rules, and conventions that are inhibiting creativity.

Saying "I'm not creative." One of the most destructive things we can do to ourselves is to believe that we cannot be creative. As discussed earlier, the Pygmalion effect can be powerful. If we believe we are not creative, we are likely to fulfill our expectations. By the same token, if we believe we can come up with novel and useful ideas, we are likely to fulfill our prophecy.

As an example of how we tend to limit our idea generation, consider the problem in Figure 7.3. One possible solution follows in Figure 7.4.

Many people have difficulty coming up with a solution because they impose constraints on the ideas they generate as workable solutions. However, often, a creative solution requires that we step outside the boundaries we perceive and view the problem from a different perspective. As long as we believe we must "stay within the box," we limit the number of practicable ideas we might develop.

Generating ideas involves escape and movement: escape from the confines of our current thinking into new realms and constant movement as we break the bonds of our current reality to seek novel connections (Plsek, 1997). We strive to find new connections, escape from early judgment and a desire to satisfice, move flexibly as we explore these novel associations, and delve into our stored concepts to expand these relationships until we are ready to harvest our more promising ideas for further processing and refinement. Improving idea generation takes time and thought. However, identifying the problem correctly and preparing ourselves with the proper resources and tools aims us in the right direction. We need to use the

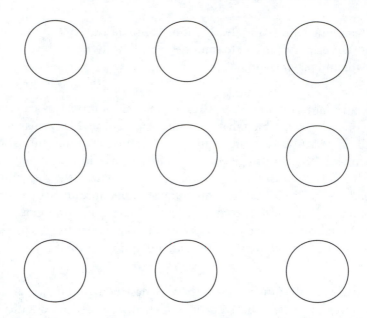

Figure 7.3. Drawing Problem: Draw three straight lines through all nine circles without lifting your pencil from the paper.

problem we identified and the tools at our disposal to direct our search. How can we solve the problem? What alternatives are available? As we consider options, we need to be aware of likely self-imposed constraints that might limit our idea search. Although habit and tradition serve well for routine problem solving, we need to break free from our reliance on the old way of doing things. We need to set challenging targets to stretch our imaginations and locate unlikely alternatives. And we need to be receptive to far-fetched possibilities by withholding judgment about how "good" the option feels. Even thoughts that seem bizarre may generate additional unexpected results. We also need to expand the number of ideas we generate. Often, we are able to "piggyback" on our suggestions by altering the context or content of an existing idea slightly by adding a new twist. When it comes to ideas, more is always better.

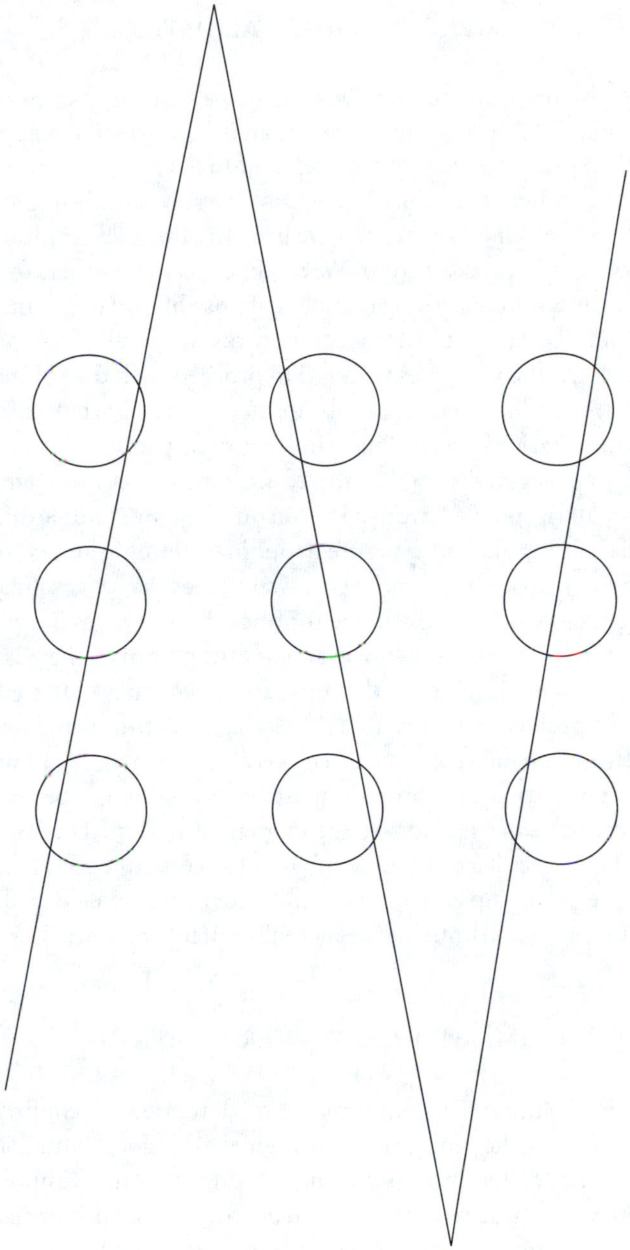

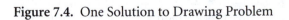

Figure 7.4. One Solution to Drawing Problem

IMPROVING IDEA VALIDATION

A creative response needs to be validated against our knowledge and other applicable criteria to assure that it is correct or appropriate (Amabile, 1988). Is the new idea useful and relevant? Will it resolve the problem identified in the initial step? Can it be successfully implemented? To improve the validation process, we need to examine our ideas to see if they survive the practicality test. We might check with others to get their input and insights concerning our ideas. If possible, we might implement the solution on a smaller scale to see if it works (by developing a prototype or model). Do the resources required to proceed with the solution exist, and if not, can additional support be located? It is important to avoid exposing our creative ideas to "black holes," those people who overwhelm us with their negativity so that the concept never sees the light of day again. Equally important, we need to run our ideas by credible others who can lend their insight and expertise to our idea, refining and tailoring the solution to meet our needs more effectively. Ideas that pass validation are compared to determine which one (or ones) best resolves our problem.

Successful idea validation involves harvesting from all the possibilities generated earlier to focus on the most attractive ones that are likely to resolve the problem we identified. Ideas that look promising need to be purposefully enhanced to strengthen possible advantages and minimize any weak points by asking probing questions. Can this idea be realistically implemented? Does it improve the current situation? Does it contain potential faults or defects? Can we predict the consequences, both short- and long-term, of implementing this idea? Remember that our ideas have little value unless and until they are actually put into action (Plsek, 1997).

IMPROVING IDEA VERIFICATION

Once the solution has been implemented, we need to confirm that it does indeed solve the problem. Did we achieve our goal? If the solution is successful, the creative process can end. In addition, what we have learned from the creative process can be applied to other similar problems. If there is complete failure, if no reasonable ideas were generated, or if implementation proved to be unsuccessful, a determination needs to be made whether to terminate the creative process (and admit that a creative solution likely does not exist) or to continue (and how to proceed). However, if progress has been achieved without complete success (generally the most likely outcome), the problem can be reformulated, and the creative process can begin again (Amabile, 1988). Signs of "getting warmer" indicate that we are on the right track, and further application of the creative process is likely to result in a new and practical resolution.

Not every problem can be solved creatively. Some problems are just too trivial or inconsequential to require creativity. Others may be too complicated or complex to resolve creatively, although the creative process is likely to lead to clarification and improved understanding of the issues at hand. A few techniques (Whetton & Cameron, 1991) that encourage flexible thinking and prepare us to think creatively include:

Giving ourselves relaxation time. Creativity is more likely when we free up our minds by breaking out of our routine. Intense work needs time out, and intense creativity requires a period of relaxation and room to breathe.

Finding a place where we can think. Sometimes, it is helpful to remove ourselves physically from the usual workplace so the creative juices can flow. Our concentration suffers when we must deal with constant interruptions. Creativity can be enhanced if we find a physical space where we are undistracted by outside influences.

Talking to others about our ideas. Identify those who stimulate your thinking processes and run your ideas by them. New perspectives bring additional insights and unforeseen possibilities. In addition, trying to explain our ideas to an outsider helps to solidify and crystallize our thinking processes. Ill-formed concepts become clearer when we are forced to communicate them to others.

Reading as much as possible. Many of us are specialized with expertise in a specific area. Cross-fertilization occurs when we branch out of our field and see how others handle their problems.

Avoiding idea killers. As mentioned previously, some people feel obligated to point out the negative and impractical aspects of ideas presented to them. Although we should expect and encourage valid criticism of our ideas, we don't want to be overwhelmed by negativity. We need to allow our ideas time and space to grow and develop. If possible, idea killers should be avoided.

Sleeping on it. Interestingly, many creative ideas have been developed while the inventor was asleep. The mind is always working, and even our unconscious and subconscious processes can assist in the incubation and development of an idea. For example, the originator of the hit game *Pac Man* (where a munching circle gobbles up dots and ghosts) developed the concept from a daydream he had while he was hungry.

ENHANCING CREATIVITY

Creative people do not necessarily think harder or smarter than others; creative thinkers are simply those who have learned methods of viewing things differently and ways of thinking that are more likely to result in desirable outcomes. They bring to bear atypical ways of seeing the problem and innovative methods of generating solutions, are well prepared with the resources required to attack the difficulty, and are motivated by the challenge and fun of the creative process itself. Creative individuals are not trapped in applying existing mental patterns but are able to move in an innovative direction toward a new (and generally untried) pattern. Plsek (1997) offers the guidelines in Table 7.3 to direct our creative processes.

SUMMARY AND REVIEW

Creativity means doing things differently: coming up with something new, relevant, and appropriate. Thinking creatively results from the application of the resources we bring to bear on the problem at hand, the techniques we use to solve problems, and the motivation we have to generate creative responses. Creativity typically follows a sequential process of five stages: Problem identification, where we come to understand the real problem; preparation, where we gather the resources needed to tackle the problem we have identified; idea generation, where we allow our minds free rein to tap into possibilities; idea validation, where we evaluate our creative ideas for practicality; and verification, where we determine if the problem has been successfully resolved.

TABLE 7.3 Guidelines to Enhance Creativity

Guideline	*Application*
Pause purposefully and notice what is going on around you	Learning to perceive the world in a fresh way increases the storehouse of knowledge available to us so we can generate more novel associations
Limit yourself to those areas you find truly interesting and focus creative energies purposefully	Work diligently over time in a specific topic area that interests you
Expand your problem definition or topic area to gain insight	Maintain the maximum amount of space needed for successful creativity
Generate original ideas by establishing new connections within your knowledge base	Be flexible and persevere by making many mental associations
Attention, escape, and movement are the fundamentals of creativity	Look at things in a new way, remove yourself from established thinking patterns, and keep moving mentally to avoid early judgment and satisficing
Pause and examine your ideas, especially those that you find humorous	Resist our urge to move on when we find something humorous and instead uncover underlying concepts that often lead to innovation
Judgments are neither right nor wrong, just patterns of response developed from experience	Avoid allowing emotions to inhibit flexibility
Harvest, develop, and act on at least some of your creative ideas	Productive innovation results from action

SOURCE: Plsek, 1997.

8 | Improving Our Decisions

Critical thinking and creative problem solving are not easy: Applying these skills requires time, resources, and effort. Not all of the problems we face require critical thinking or creativity. However, we are likely to improve the quality of our important decisions if we practice critical thinking skills and creative problem-solving techniques. Realizing how decisions are actually made and understanding the factors influencing our decision making provide knowledge and awareness of possible constraints that can contaminate and inhibit our thinking processes.

Usually, we strive to be rational, to make the best possible decision all the time. Unfortunately, human decision makers are subject to bounded rationality, which restricts our ability to optimize decisions. In spite of this, our decisions can still approach the optimal if we are aware of how decisions should be made as well as what elements influence our judgments. Our decisional processes are driven by biological factors that influence how we think and what we do. Mechanisms that are in place to ensure our survival also interfere with our ability to think rationally. Chemical bodily reactions to environmental conditions determine to a large extent what we believe is important and meaningful; often, the major decisions in our lives invoke strong physical responses. Physiological reactions brought on by our appraisal of our surroundings give rise to our emotions, and our emotions direct our attention. Emotions can often overwhelm our reasoning, taking possession of our desire to be logical and reasonable. The primitive parts of the brain can have an overpowering impact on our decisions unless we consciously focus our attention on what is truly important and allow the thinking and problem-solving portions of our mind to take charge of our decision making.

Our emotional nature drives us to be impulsive, to do what we want rather than what we should. However, our hotheaded side can be curtailed and contained if we force ourselves to consider a full spectrum of possibilities rather than perceiving decision making as one option at a time. When confronted with an issue, our problem solving improves if we expand the number of alternatives we are contemplating (Anderson, 1982). Additional possibilities allow us to remove the immediacy derived from our wants and focus on future well-being and long-term benefits. In decision making, more (options, alternatives, objectives, ideas, and so forth) is always better. We need to be aware of and give credence to our impulsive nature; otherwise, it may simply take charge at the time of the decision. If we understand the emotions that are impelling us in an impulsive direction and figure out what we can do to address or at least partially satisfy our compulsive side, we can apply a more reasoned response to our problems. When we avoid considering options one at a time and expand our possibilities, we remove (or at least lessen) the likelihood that our immediate short-term needs will outweigh our more rational long-term desires.

A number of judgmental biases can affect our ability to think critically and solve problems creatively. Humans often fall prey to selective perception; we see what we expect as well as what we want to see. To minimize this effect, we need to be aware of our own motivation to perceive things in a certain way, understand what expectations we bring to the situation, and decide whether our perception of the problem would vary if our motives and expectations were changed. Impression effects such as primacy, recency, and halo demonstrate that our view of the problem can be biased by when we receive relevant information and how we pigeonhole the facts we use to make our decisions. How information comes to us influences our thoughts. The information-processing center of the mind seeks out any data that may be useful, latches onto perceived facts (even if they are irrelevant), and often fails to adjust sufficiently from an established anchor point. In addition, how we frame a problem influences our subsequent choice: Positively framed situations lead us to avoid risk and play it safe, whereas negatively framed problems motivate us to seek risk and take the gamble. Although these judgmental biases cannot be completely eliminated, awareness that we are susceptible to their influences is the first step toward minimizing their impact on our decisions. Furthermore, one of the most effective techniques that has been found to reduce errors in judgment is simply expanding the way we view things and considering additional alternatives (Anderson, 1982; Lord, Lepper, & Preston, 1984). Objective consideration of divergent perspectives and additional alternatives will almost always improve the quality of judgment and decision making (Plous, 1993).

Continuing to support a failing course of action (escalation of commitment) can also bias our decisions unless we set limits (and stick to them) prior to entering into a potential escalation situation. Furthermore, we can avoid the tendency to escalate if we are able to diffuse and spread responsibility for any initial investment decision. Also, the way the mind categorizes and uses stored information determines the accuracy of the resources available for problem resolution. Categorization effects such as representativeness (the tendency to believe something is a typical example), regression to the mean (the tendency for extreme examples to be followed by more average or realistic outcomes), and availability (the tendency to recall events that are more vivid, easily imagined, or emotionally laden) demonstrate that the way we access, retrieve, and use information stored in memory can weaken our decisional accuracy. Most of the time, data accessed from memory and used in problem solving produces reasonably accurate decisions. However, we need to be aware that the way the human mind categorizes and uses information can also lead to systematic erroneous judgments.

Our perceptions of risk can also influence how we make decisions. Risk varies depending on how much uncertainty we believe is present, whether gains and losses are large or small, how we frame the risk situation, and how personally involved we will be with the outcome. These factors determine how risky we believe a decision will be and how much control we think we have over the final outcome of our decision. To the extent that we are able to decrease the amount of uncertainty we feel, we believe the gains we will achieve offset possible losses, we view situations in both positive and negative terms to avoid framing distortions, and we believe we will not be held personally responsible (and possibly punished) for potential negative outcomes resulting from a risky decision, perceptions of risk diminish. However, our perceptions of risk increase when the opposite is true, and we are less likely to decide in favor of pursuing a risky course of action. Understanding the elements of risk and how they affect our thinking improves our decision making.

Critical thinking requires an open yet skeptical mind. We must be willing to consider new information and ways of doing things, but we must also skeptically scrutinize what we hear as well as what we believe. As we think about various claims and weigh the evidence, we need to consider the source, look at possible alternative explanations, and test what we hear (and what we believe) to determine the truthfulness of information. Believability increases when the source of what we hear is credible (although we must be aware that even trustworthy information sources can be misinformed or simply dead wrong). Believability also increases when we have determined that possible alternate explanations are not as likely to be true as the new information we are considering. And believability increases when we are able to test the evidence and determine for ourselves the truthfulness of what we are asked to accept.

Creativity occurs when we come up with something new and useful. Creativity is much more likely to take place when we have abundant personal resources available for problem solving, we apply appropriate techniques and processes during the creative process, and we are internally motivated by the challenge inherent in the problem we face. Attention to each of the five steps or stages of the creative process can increase the likelihood that a novel and relevant outcome will result. The most important aspect of problem identification is to make sure we are identifying the real problem; recognizing the actual problem sets the stage for how effective subsequent steps will be. Preparation can be improved if we supplement our existing knowledge base with appropriate materials and resources that can assist with our understanding and perspective toward the situation at hand. Idea generation is where true creativity usually occurs. It is here that novel, different, and original material comes into existence. During idea generation, we must not allow ourselves to be artificially constrained by self-imposed boundaries, we must challenge as many assumptions as possible, and we must alter our vantage point to see things from as many angles as possible. The ideas we develop are then validated during the fourth phase of the creative process. Is our new idea truly practical? Can it be implemented successfully? Finally, we verify if the creative solution lives up to our expectations. Does the solution resolve the problem? Are we at least getting closer to resolution? Should we continue the process, and if so, how?

The resources (our experience and knowledge) we bring to the creative process provide the foundation on which we build our ideas. The more relevant information we have access to, the greater our opportunity to combine and reframe the various pieces to develop something creative. If we don't have enough resources to draw from, we can acquire additional raw materials from various sources such as knowledgeable others or established databases. A lack of necessary information may take time to rectify, but it can be addressed. Having too much experience, however, often leads us to use old and familiar ways of looking at the problem and historical methods of dealing with it. Creative individuals are those who apply innovative and appropriate thinking skills during the analytical process. It is our ability to gain a new perspective, to challenge our assumptions, to break perceived boundaries and rules, and to change the way we view both the problem and the possible ways to resolve it that makes the creative difference. Applying processes that enable and allow us to "be creative" is what separates merely competent decision makers from creative ones. However, even when the necessary skills and resources are present and we have access to and can apply creative thinking techniques, creativity will suffer if we are not motivated to be creative. Unless being in the creative process itself challenges us and we perceive the hunt for a creative solution as fun and interesting, we will not devote the time and energy needed to develop something original and practical.

It is unlikely that we will ever be able to completely eliminate the judgmental errors that occur when we make decisions. People are not computers with perfect algorithms. The amazing human brain, the most complicated and advanced three pounds of matter in the universe, is still limited by the biological constraints of its human carrying case, by limits in information processing, and by external forces such as deadlines and expectations. However, we can still improve the quality of the decisions we make by being aware of how systematic biases influence our judgments. If we recognize that we are susceptible to judgmental errors, we can then take steps to minimize or avoid them.

Furthermore, decision making is improved if we apply critical thinking skills to the problems we face. Why do we believe what we believe? What evidence is required to convince us to change our mind and adopt a new belief system? We need to be open to new information but to question everything, even our deeply held convictions. Our beliefs determine how we will decide and what we will do, so we must be sure that what we believe is as close to the truth as we can get. How good is the evidence? Is the source credible? Does another explanation work as well or better? How can we test the new concept to see if it is valid? Important decisions require well-substantiated beliefs.

Finally, creativity occurs when resources, techniques, and motivation are high. If we lack proper resources, we must search until we find a necessary and sufficient foundation from which to work. If we apply creative techniques such as reformulating the problem and its various solutions, looking at all aspects from as many different angles as possible and allowing ourselves to be uninhibited and to have fun, then we are much more likely to generate something new and useful. And if we are motivated by the interest, enjoyment, satisfaction, and challenge of the problem (and the creative process) itself, we will be more willing to invest the time and energy required to bring about creativity.

References

Adler, N. J. (1997). *International dimensions of organizational behavior* (3rd ed.). Cincinnati, OH: International Thomson.

Ainslie, G. (1992). *Picoeconomics: The interaction of successive motivational states within the individual.* New York: Cambridge University Press.

Allen, J. L. (1974). *Conceptual blockbusting.* San Francisco: Freeman.

Allport, G. W., & Postman, L. J. (1947). *The psychology of rumor.* New York: Holt.

Amabile, T. M. (1988). A model of creativity and innovation in organizations. *Research in Organizational Behavior, 10,* 123-167.

Amabile, T. M. (1997). Motivating creativity in organizations: On doing what you love and loving what you do. *California Management Review, 40,* 39-58.

Amit, R., & Wernerfelt, B. (1990). Why do firms reduce business risks? *Academy of Management Journal, 33,* 520-533.

Anderson, C. A. (1982). Inoculation and counterexplanation: Debiasing techniques in the perseverance of social theories. *Social Cognition, 1,* 126-139.

Arkes, H. R., & Blumer, C. (1985). The psychology of sunk costs. *Organizational Behavior and Human Decision Processes, 35,* 124-140.

Asch, S. E. (1946). Forming impressions of personality. *Journal of Abnormal and Social Psychology, 41,* 258-290.

Asch, S. E. (1956). Studies of independence and conformity: A minority of one against a unanimous majority. *Psychological Monographs, 70,* 9.

Barron, F. B., & Harrington, D. M. (1981). Creativity, intelligence, and personality. *Annual Review of Psychology, 32,* 439-476.

Bazerman, M. H. (1990). *Judgment in managerial decision making.* New York: John Wiley.

Bazerman, M. H., Beekun, R. I., & Schoorman, F. D. (1982). Performance evaluation in a dynamic context: The impact of a prior commitment to the ratee. *Journal of Applied Psychology, 67,* 873-876.

Bazerman, M. H., Schroth, H., Pradhan, P., Diekmann, K., & Tenbrunsel, A. (1994). The inconsistent role of comparison others and procedural justice in reactions to hypothetical job descriptions: Implications for job acceptance decisions. *Organizational Behavior and Human Decision Processes, 60,* 326-352.

Bazerman, M. H., Tenbrunsel, A. E., & Wade-Benzoni, K. (1998). Negotiating with yourself and losing: Making decisions with competing internal preferences. *Academy of Management Journal, 23,* 225-241.

Beach, L. R. (1990). *Image theory: Decision making in personal and organizational contexts.* New York: John Wiley.

Bem, D. B. (1972). Self-perception theory. In L. Berkowitz (Ed.), *Advances in experimental social psychology* (Vol. 6). New York: Academic Press.

Bobocel, D. R., & Meyer, J. P. (1994). Escalating commitment to a failing course of action: Separating the roles of choice and justification. *Journal of Applied Psychology, 79,* 360-363.

Brigham, T. A. (1979). Some effects of choice on academic performance. In L. C. Perlmuter & R. A. Monty (Eds.), *Choice and perceived control.* Hillsdale, NJ: Lawrence Erlbaum.

Brookfield, S. (1987). *Critical thinkers.* San Francisco: Jossey-Bass.

Bruner, J. A., & Postman, L. (1949). On the perception of incongruity: A paradigm. *Journal of Personality, 18,* 206-223.

Chandler, W. R. (1948). The relationship of distance to the occurrence of pedestrian accidents. *Sociometry, 11,* 108-113.

Christensen-Szalanski, J. J. J. (1984). Discount functions and the measurement of patients' values: Women's decisions during childbirth. *Medical Decision Making, 4,* 47-58.

Combs, B., & Slovic, P. (1979). Newspaper coverage of causes of death. *Journalism Quarterly, 56,* 843-847, 849.

Conlisk, J. (1996). Why bounded rationality? *Journal of Economic Literature, 34,* 669-700.

Conlon, D. E., & Garland, H. (1993). The role of project completion information in resource allocation decisions. *Academy of Management Journal, 36,* 402-413.

Cooper, J., & Croyle, R. T. (1984). Attitudes and attitude change. *Annual Review of Psychology, 35,* 395-426.

Cowan, D. A. (1986). Developing a process model of problem recognition. *Academy of Management Review, 11,* 763-776.

Crocker, J. (1981). Judgment of covariation by social perceivers. *Psychological Bulletin, 90,* 272-292.

Csikszentmihalyi, M. (1997). Happiness and creativity. *Futurist, 31,* 8-12.

Darke, P. R., & Freedman, J. L. (1993). Deciding whether to seek a bargain: Effects of both amount and percent off. *Journal of Applied Psychology, 78,* 960-965.

Dawes, R. M. (1988). *Rational choice in an uncertain world.* New York: Harcourt Brace Jovanovich.

Dawkins, R. (1986). *The blind watchmaker.* London: Norton.

Dion, K., Berscheid, E., & Walster, E. (1972). What is beautiful is good. *Journal of Personality and Social Psychology, 24,* 285-290.

Dougherty, T. W., Turban, D. B., & Callender, J. C. (1994). Confirming first impressions in the employment interview: A field study of interviewer behavior. *Journal of Applied Psychology, 79,* 659-665.

Drucker, P. F. (1954). *The practice of management.* New York: Harper & Row.

Dunegan, K. J. (1995). Image theory: Testing the role of image compatibility in progress decisions. *Organizational Behavior and Human Decision Processes, 62,* 79-86.

Einhorn, H. J., & Hogarth, R. M. (1977). Confidence in judgment: Persistence of the illusion of validity. *Psychological Review, 85,* 395-416.

Fazio, R. H., & Zanna, M. P. (1978). On the predictive validity of attitudes: The roles of direct experience and confidence. *Journal of Personality, 46,* 228-243.

Fogler, H. S., & LeBlanc, S. E. (1995). *Strategies for creative problem solving.* Upper Saddle River, New Jersey: Prentice Hall.

Frank, M. G., & Gilovich, T. (1988). The dark side of self and social perception: Black uniforms and aggression in professional sports. *Journal of Personality and Social Psychology, 54,* 74-85.

Frisch, D. (1993). Reasons for framing effects. *Organizational Behavior and Human Decision Processes, 54,* 399-429.

Gazzaniga, M. (1985). *The social brain.* New York: Basic Books.

Gazzaniga, M. (1988). *Mind matters: How mind and brain interact to create our conscious limits.* Boston: Houghton Mifflin.

Giere, R. N. (1997). *Understanding scientific reasoning.* Fort Worth, TX: Harcourt Brace.

Gilovich, T. (1987). Secondhand information and social judgment. *Journal of Experimental Social Psychology, 23,* 59-74.

Gilovich, T. (1993). *How we know what isn't so: The fallibility of human reason in everyday life.* New York: Free Press.

Gilovich, T., Vallone, R., & Tversky, A. (1985). The hot hand in basketball: On the misperception of random sequences. *Journal of Personality and Social Psychology, 17,* 295-314.

Gordon, W. J. J. (1961). *Synectics: The development of creative capacity.* New York: Collier.

Greenberg, J., Williams, K. D., & O'Brien, M. K. (1986). Considering the harshest verdict first: Biasing effects on mock juror verdicts. *Personality and Social Psychology Bulletin, 12,* 41-50.

Halpern, D. F. (1998). Teaching critical thinking for transfer across domains: Dispositions, skills, structure training, and metacognitive monitoring. *American Psychologist, 53,* 449-455.

Higgins, J. M. (1994). Creating creativity. *Training & Development, 48,* 11-15.

Highhouse, S., & Yuce, P. (1996). Perspectives, perceptions, and risk-taking behavior. *Organizational Behavior and Human Decision Processes, 65,* 159-167.

Hobson, J. A. (1994). *The chemistry of conscious states: How the brain changes its mind.* Boston: Little, Brown.

Hogarth, R. (1980). *Judgment and choice.* Chichester, UK: Wiley.

Hunter, I. M. L. (1964). *Memory.* Middlesex, UK: Penguin.

Janis, I. L. (1982). *Groupthink: Psychological studies of policy decisions and fiascos.* Boston: Houghton Mifflin.

Kahneman, D., & Tversky, A. (1973). On the psychology of prediction. *Psychological Review, 80,* 251-273.

Kelley, H. H. (1950). The warm-cold variable in first impressions of persons. *Journal of Personality, 18,* 431-439.

Kepner, C. H., & Tregoe, B. B. (1981). *The new rational manager.* Princeton, NJ: Princeton Research Press.

Kimmelberg, H., & Norenberg, M. (1989). Astrocytes. *Scientific American,* 66-76.

Kirschenbaum, S. S. (1992). Influence of experience on information-gathering strategies. *Journal of Applied Psychology, 77,* 343-352.

Klayman, J., & Ha, Y. (1987). Confirmation, disconfirmation, and information in hypothesis testing. *Psychological Review, 94,* 211-228.

Kolb, B., & Milner, B. (1981). Performance of complex arm and facial movements after focal brain lesions. *Neuropsychologia, 19,* 505-514.

Landy, D., & Sigall, H. (1974). Beauty is talent: Task evaluation as a function of the performer's physical attractiveness. *Journal of Personality and Social Psychology, 32,* 311-328.

Langer, E. J. (1975). The illusion of control. *Journal of Personality and Social Psychology, 32,* 311-328.

Langer, E., & Schank, R. C. (1994). *Beliefs, reasoning, and decision making.* Hillsdale, NJ: Lawrence Erlbaum.

LeDoux, J. E. (1994). Emotion, memory, and brain. *Scientific American, 270,* 50-57.

Lerner, M. J. (1970). The desire for justice and reaction to victims. In J. R. Macaulay & L. Berkowitz (Eds.), *Altruism and helping behavior.* New York: Academic Press.

Levin, I. P. (1987). Associative effects of information framing. *Bulletin of the Psychonomic Society, 25,* 85-86.

Levin, I. P., & Gaeth, G. J. (1988). Framing of attribute information before and after consuming the product. *Journal of Consumer Research, 15,* 374-378.

Levinthal, C. F. (1988). *Messengers of paradise: Opiates and the brain.* New York: Anchor Press.

Lister, P. (1992, July). A skeptics guide to psychics. *Redbook,* pp. 103-105, 112-113.

Locke, E. A., & Latham, G. P. (1988). The determinants of goal commitment. *Academy of Management Review, 13,* 23-39.

Loewenstein, G. (1996). Out of control: Visceral influences on behavior. *Organizational Behavior and Human Decision Processes, 65,* 272-292.

Loftus, E. (1980). *Memory: Surprising new insights into how we remember and why we forget.* New York: Ardsley House.

Lord, C. G., Lepper, M. R., & Preston, E. (1984). Considering the opposite: A corrective strategy for social judgment. *Journal of Personality and Social Psychology, 47,* 1231-1243.

Lowenthal, D. (1993). *Reversal of preference in candidate choice.* Unpublished manuscript, Carnegie Mellon University, Pittsburgh, PA.

Lumsden, C. J., & Findlay, C. S. (1988). Evolution of the creative mind. *Creativity Research Journal, 1,* 75-91.

Lutz, W. (1989). *Doublespeak: From "revenue enhancement" to "terminal living"—How government, business, advertisers, and others use language to deceive you.* New York: Harper & Row.

MacCrimmon, K. R., & Wehrung, D. A. (1986). *Taking risks: The management of uncertainty.* New York: Free Press.

Maier, N. R. F. (1970). *Problem solving and creativity in individuals and groups.* Belmont, CA: Cole.

March, J. G. (1994). *A primer on decision making.* New York: Free Press.

March, J. G., & Shapira, Z. (1987). Managerial perspectives on risk and risk taking. *Management Science, 33,* 1404-1418.

March, J., & Simon, H. (1958). *Organizations.* New York: John Wiley.

Martin, E. B. (1981). The conspicuous consumption of rhinos. *Animal Kingdom, 84,* 20-29.

McGuire, W. J. (1964). Inducing resistance to persuasion. In L. Berkowitz (Ed.), *Advances in experimental social psychology.* New York: Academic Press.

Miller, G. A. (1956). The magical number seven, plus or minus two: Some limits on our capacity for processing information. *Psychological Review, 63,* 81-97.

Miller, N., & Campbell, D. T. (1959). Recency and primacy in persuasion as a function of the timing of speeches and measurements. *Journal of Abnormal and Social Psychology, 59,* 1-9.

Mintzberg, H. (1975). *The nature of managerial work.* New York: Harper & Row.

Mitroff, I. (1998). *Smart thinking for crazy times.* San Francisco: Berrett-Koehler.

Moreland, R. L., & Zajonc, R. B. (1979). Exposure effects may not depend on stimulus recognition. *Journal of Personality and Social Psychology, 37,* 1085-1089.

Myers, D. G. (1990). *Social psychology.* New York: McGraw-Hill.

Nisbett, R. E., & Ross, L. (1980). *Human inference: Strategies and shortcomings of social judgment.* Englewood Cliffs, NJ: Prentice Hall.

Nisbett, R. E., & Smith, M. (1989). Predicting interpersonal attraction from small samples: A reanalysis of Newcomb's acquaintance study. *Social Cognition, 7,* 67-73.

Northcraft, G. B., & Neale, M. A. (1987). Experts, amateurs, and real estate: An anchoring-and-adjustment perspective on property pricing decisions. *Organizational Behavior and Human Decision Processes, 39,* 84-97.

Northcraft, G. B., & Wolf, G. (1984). Dollars, sense, and sunk costs: A life cycle model of resource allocation decisions. *Academy of Management Review, 9,* 225-234.

Novitt-Moreno, A. D. (1995). *How your brain works.* Emeryville, CA: Ziff-Davis.

Nowlis, S. M., & Simonson, I. (1997). Attribute-task compatibility as a determinant of consumer preference reversals. *Journal of Marketing Research, 34,* 205-218.

Oldham, G. R., & Cummings, A. (1996). Employee creativity: Personal and contextual factors at work. *Academy of Management Journal, 39,* 607-634.

Osborn, A. F. (1953). *Applied imagination.* New York: Scribner.

Peters, T. J., & Waterman, R. H. (1982). *In search of excellence.* New York: Warner.

Pitz, G. F., & Sachs, N. J. (1984). Judgment and decision: Theory and application. *Annual Review of Psychology, 35,* 139-163.

Plous, S. (1993). *The psychology of judgment and decision making.* New York: McGraw-Hill.

Plsek, P. E. (1997). *Creativity, innovation, and quality.* Milwaukee, WI: ASQC Quality Press.

Power, D. J., & Aldag, R. J. (1985). Soelberg's job search and choice model: A clarification, review, and critique. *Academy of Management Review, 10,* 48-58.

Quattrone, G. A., Lawrence, C. P., Warren, D. L., Souza-Silva, K., Finkel, S. E., & Andrus, D. E. (1984). *Explorations in anchoring: The effects of prior range, anchor extremity, and suggestive hints.* Unpublished manuscript, Stanford University, Stanford, CA.

Quattrone, G. A., & Tversky, A. (1988). Contrasting rational and psychological analyses of political choice. *American Political Science Review, 82,* 719-736.

Ritov, I., & Kahneman, D. (1997). How people value the environment. In M. H. Bazerman, D. M. Messick, A. E. Tenbrunsel, & K. A. Wade-Benzoni (Eds.), *Environment, ethics, and behavior.* San Francisco: New Lexington Press.

Roethlisberger, F. J., & Dickson, W. J. (1939). *Management and the worker: An account of a research program conducted by the Western Electric Company, Hawthorne Works, Chicago.* Cambridge, MA: Harvard University Press.

Rosenberg, M. J., & Hovland, C. I. (1960). Cognitive, affective, and behavioral components of attitude. In M. J. Rosenberg, C. I. Hovland, W. J. McGuire, R. P. Abelson, & J. H. Brehm (Eds.), *Attitude, organization, and change.* New Haven, CT: Yale University Press.

Rosenthal, R. (1987). Pygmalion effects: Existence, magnitude, and social importance. *Educational Researcher,* pp. 37-41.

Ross, J., & Staw, B. M. (1986). Expo '86: An escalation prototype. *Administrative Science Quarterly, 31,* 274-297.

Rothenburg, A. (1979). Creative contradictions. *Psychology Today, 13,* 55-62.

Rubin, J. Z. (1980). Experimental research on third party intervention in conflict: Toward some generalizations. *Psychological Bulletin, 87,* 379-391.

Ruchlis, H. (1991). *How do you know it's true?* Buffalo, NY: Prometheus.

Rudinow, J., & Barry, V. E. (1994). *Invitation to critical thinking.* Fort Worth, TX: Harcourt Brace.

Russo, J. E., & Schoemaker, P. J. H. (1989). *Decision traps: Ten barriers to brilliant decision making and how to overcome them.* New York: Simon & Schuster.

Schaubroeck, J., & Williams, S. (1993). Type A behavior and escalating commitment. *Journal of Applied Psychology, 78,* 862-867.

Selye, H. (1956). *The stress of life.* New York: McGraw-Hill.

Shanteau, J. (1992). The psychology of experts: An alternative view. In G. Wright & F. Bolger (Eds.), *Expertise and decision support.* New York: Plenum.

Sill, D. J. (1996). Integrative thinking, synthesis, and creativity in interdisciplinary studies. *Journal of General Education, 45,* 129-151.

Simon, H. A. (1957). *Models of man.* New York: John Wiley.

Simon, H. (1967). Motivational and emotional controls of cognition. *Psychological Review, 74,* 29-39.

Simon, H. (1978). Information-processing theory of human problem-solving. In W. K. Estes (Ed.), *Handbook of learning and cognitive processes: Vol. 5. Human information processing.* Hillsdale, NJ: Lawrence Erlbaum.

Simon, H. A. (1987). Making management decisions: The role of intuition and emotion. *Academy of Management Executives, 1,* 57-64.

Simon, H. A. (1990). Invariants of human behavior. *Annual Review of Psychology, 41,* 1-19.

Sitkin, S. B., & Pablo, A. L. (1992). Reconceptualizing the determinants of risk behavior. *Academy of Management Review, 17,* 9-38.

Slovic, P., & Lichtenstein, S. (1971). Comparison of Bayesian and regression approaches in the study of information processing in judgment. *Organizational Behavior and Human Decision Processes, 6,* 649-744.

Snyder, M., & Cantor, N. (1979). Testing hypotheses about other people: The use of historical knowledge. *Journal of Experimental Social Psychology, 15,* 330-342.

Staw, B. M. (1976). Knee-deep in the big muddy: A study of escalating commitment to a chosen course of action. *Organizational Behavior and Human Decision Processes, 16,* 27-44.

Staw, B. M., & Ross, J. (1987). Behavior in escalation situations: Antecedents, prototypes, and solution. *Research in Organizational Behavior, 9,* 39-78.

Stein, B. S. (1989). Memory and creativity. In J. A. Glover, R. R. Ronning, & C. R. Reynolds (Eds.), *Handbook of creativity* (pp. 163-176). New York: Plenum.

Strickland, L. (1958). Surveillance and trust. *Journal of Personality, 26,* 200-215.

Strickland, L., Lewicki, R. J., & Katz, A. M. (1966). Temporal orientation and perceived control as determinants of risk taking. *Journal of Experimental Social Psychology, 2,* 143-151.

Svenson, O. (1981). Are we all less risky and more skillful than our fellow drivers? *Acta Psychologica, 47,* 143-148.

Swinyard, W. (1982). The interaction between comparative advertising and copy-claim variation. *Journal of Marketing Research, 18,* 173-186.

Sylwester, R. (1995). *A celebration of neurons.* Alexandria, VA: Association for Supervision and Curriculum Development.

Tetlock, P. E., Sitka, L., & Boettger, R. (1989). Social and cognitive strategies for coping with accountability: Conformity, complexity, and bolstering. *Journal of Economic Behavior and Organization, 1,* 39-60.

Thaler, R. (1980). Toward a positive theory of consumer choice. *Journal of Economic Behavior and Organization, 1,* 39-80.

Thaler, R., & Shefrin, H. M. (1981). An economic theory of self-control. *Journal of Political Economy, 89,* 392-406.

Thorndike, E. L. (1920). A constant error in psychological ratings. *Journal of Applied Psychology, 4,* 25-29.

Tice, D. M., Bratslavsky, E., & Baumeister, R. F. (2001). Emotional distress regulation takes precedence over impulse control: If you feel bad, do it! *Journal of Personality and Social Psychology, 80,* 53-67.

Treffinger, D. J., & Gowan, J. C. (1971). An updated representative list of methods and educational programs for stimulating creativity. *Journal of Creative Behavior, 5,* 127-139.

Trow, C. E. (1905). *The old shipmasters of Salem.* New York: Macmillan.

Tversky, A., & Kahneman, D. (1971). Belief in the law of small numbers. *Psychological Bulletin, 76,* 105-110.

Tversky, A., & Kahneman, D. (1973). Availability: A heuristic for judging frequency and probability. *Cognitive Psychology, 5,* 207-232.

Tversky, A., & Kahneman, D. (1974). Judgment under uncertainty: Heuristics and biases. *Science, 185,* 1124-1131.

Tversky, A., & Kahneman, D. (1981). The framing of decisions and the psychology of choice. *Science, 211,* 453-458.

Tversky, A., & Kahneman, D. (1982). Judgments of and by representativeness. In D. Kahneman, P. Slovic, & A. Tversky (Eds.), *Judgment under uncertainty: Heuristics and biases.* Cambridge, UK: Cambridge University Press.

Vallone, R. P., Ross, L., & Lepper, M. R. (1985). The hostile media phenomenon: Biased perception and perceptions of media bias in coverage of the Beirut massacre. *Journal of Personality and Social Psychology, 49,* 577-585.

Vincent, J. D. (1990). *The biology of emotions* (J. Hughes, Trans.). Cambridge, MA: Basil Blackwell.

Von Oech, R. (1990). *A whack on the side of the head.* New York: Warner.

Vos Savant, M. (1996). *The power of logical thinking.* New York: St. Martin's.

Wagner, R. K. (1997). Intelligence, training, and employment. *American Psychologist, 52,* 1059-1069.

Wallas, G. (1926). *The art of thought.* New York: Harcourt.

Walsh, V. (1996). *Rationality, allocation, and reproduction.* Oxford, UK: Clarendon Press.

Ward, R. A., & Grasha, A. F. (1986). Using astrology to teach research methods to introductory psychology students. *Teaching of Psychology, 13,* 143-145.

Wason, P. C. (1960). On the failure to eliminate hypotheses in a conceptual task. *Quarterly Journal of Experimental Psychology, 12,* 129-140.

Whetton, D. A., & Cameron, K. S. (1991). *Developing management skills.* New York: HarperCollins.

Whyte, G. (1991). Diffusion of responsibility: Effects on the escalation tendency. *Journal of Applied Psychology, 76,* 408-415.

Williams, S. (1990). *The effects of choice of rewards upon individual behaviors and attitudes.* Unpublished doctoral dissertation, University of Nebraska–Lincoln.

Williams, S. (1998). An organizational model of choice: A theoretical analysis differentiating choice, personal control, and self-determination. *Genetic, Social, and General Psychology Monographs, 124,* 465-491.

Williams, S., & Luthans, F. (1992). The impact of choice of rewards and feedback on task performance. *Journal of Organizational Behavior, 13,* 653-666.

Williams, S., & Wong, T. S. (1999). Mood and organizational citizenship behavior: The effects of positive affect on employee organizational citizenship behavior intentions. *Journal of Psychology: Interdisciplinary and Applied, 133,* 656-668.

Williams, S., & Wong, Y. (1999). The effects of mood on managerial risk perceptions: Exploring affect and the dimensions of risk. *Journal of Social Psychology, 139,* 268-287.

Wilson, D. K., Kaplan, R. M., & Schneiderman, L. J. (1987). Framing of decisions and selection of alternatives in health care. *Social Behaviour, 2,* 51-59.

Woodman, R. W., Sawyer, J. E., & Griffin, R. W. (1993). Toward a theory of organizational creativity. *Academy of Management Review, 18,* 293-321.

Word, C. O., Zanna, M. P., & Cooper, J. (1974). The nonverbal mediation of self-fulfilling prophecies in interracial interaction. *Journal of Experimental Social Psychology, 10,* 109-120.

Word watch. (1989). *Chance: New Directions for Statistics and Computing, 2,* 5.

Wright, W. F., & Bower, G. H. (1992). Mood effects on subjective probability assessment. *Organizational Behavior and Human Decision Processes, 52,* 276-291.

Wylie, R. C. (1979). *The self-concept: Theory and research on selected topics.* Lincoln: University of Nebraska Press.

Yates, J. F., & Stone, E. R. (1992). The risk construct. In J. F. Yates (Ed.), *Risk-taking behavior* (pp. 1-25). Chichester, UK: Wiley.

Index

About the Author

Steve Williams is Professor of Management, Assistant Dean, and former Director for the Center for Entrepreneurship and Executive Development at Texas Southern University. He graduated summa cum laude from Metropolitan State University in Colorado and received his Ph.D. in organizational behavior at the University of Nebraska.

Williams teaches courses in organizational behavior, critical thinking and creative problem solving, international management, and strategic management, and he has published more than 20 articles in prominent journals such as the *Journal of Applied Psychology, Journal of Organizational Behavior, Journal of Applied Social Psychology,* and others. His research interests include managerial risk behavior, the effects of mood on decision making, and creative problem solving. Williams received the 2001 Teaching Excellence Award from the Jesse H. Jones School of Business, as well as teaching commendations from the National University of Singapore.

Williams has presented seminars and consulted for the Singapore Institute of Personnel Management, the Central Provident Fund of Singapore, Malayan Banking Berhad, and other firms in the United States and in Southeast Asia in the areas of motivation, managerial decision making, and creative problem solving.